American Classic

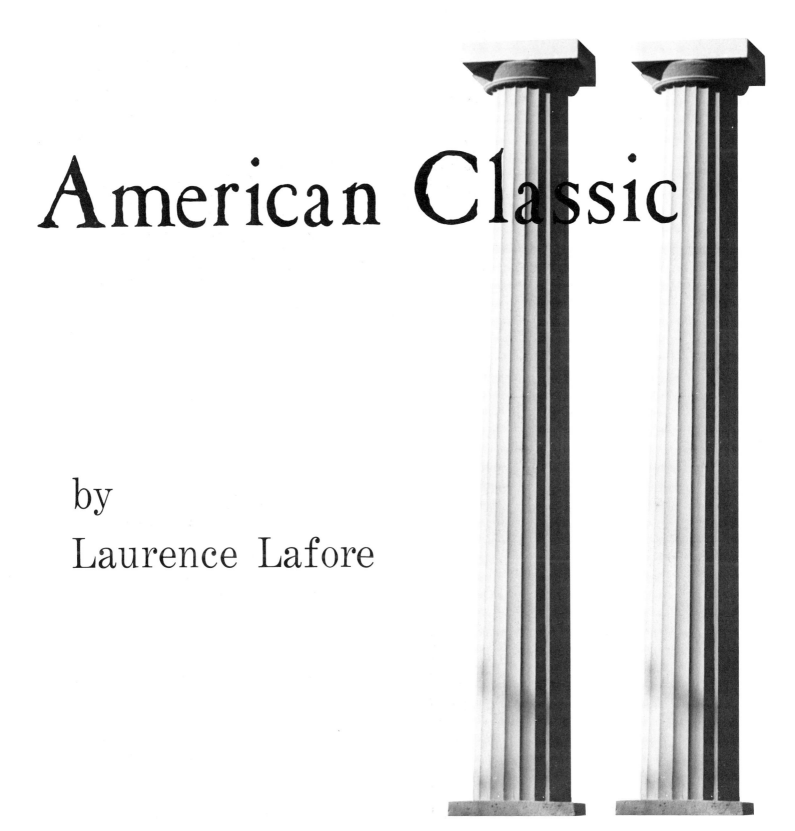

by

Laurence Lafore

Iowa State Historical Department/Division of the State Historical Society

First edition

Library of Congress Cataloging in Publication Data:

Lafore, Laurence Davis.
    American classic

        1. Architecture — Iowa City. I Title.
NA735.I58L33   917.77'65   75-9698
ISBN 0-89033-001-8

Preface

The word "classic" needs explanation. It means quite a lot of different things.

"Classic" comes from the Latin word classis, one of the groups into which ancient Romans were divided for purposes of taxation—something like a "tax bracket" for Americans. It became the modern word "class," and the adjective "classic" first referred to the higher tax brackets, the richest or the best. Then it came to mean, also, a leader not only in quality but in time, someone or something that served as a model. From that it came to mean "typical" or "representative" of a group of like things, and then, rather carelessly, people began to use it merely to mean notable, as when sportscasters talk about the Sugar Bowl as a "football classic."

"Classic" also refers to the civilization of ancient Greece and Rome. "Classical times" were a period of something like a 1000 years, in about the middle of which the birth of Christ took place, when Greek and Roman cultures were at their height. This use first appeared in English (in the year 1613) at a time when Greeks and Romans were judged (correctly) to have achieved levels of excellence never equaled before or since, and their works were regarded as models to be imitated and as standards against which to measure modern attainments.

In this book the word "classic" is used in several of these senses: Iowa City as representative of the way American towns were planned and grew; Iowa City as an exemplar of the decisive and pervasive influence of Greek and Roman ideals in American Life; and in a way that would have been intelligible to people in the seventeenth century, as the opposite of the word "Gothic." In times when "classic" meant civilized and excellent, "Gothic" was being used as a synonym for barbaric, to describe those medieval times when the West had incontinently neglected the Greek and Roman heritage. Grant Wood thought Midwestern civilization might be seen as Gothic; it must also be seen as classic.

This book is presented to readers with the hope that it may entertain and perhaps instruct them by showing and telling something about some buildings in Iowa City. But it is about much more than just buildings: it is about our past, present, and future, about our ancestors, ourselves, and our heirs. For buildings are the genes of a community, the die-stamps that people and generations imprint on their successors.

It is only a fragment. I have left out much I should have put in if I were not aware of the simple fact, so often difficult for writers to grasp, that if you do not stop sometime you will go on forever. Some other things were left out for technical reasons—quite a lot of buildings, particularly those that face north and have a lot of shrubbery around them, are virtually unphotographable. Some were left out for reasons of theme —I have tried to tell a story, and some interesting buildings simply do not fit into the plot. Some were left out because, although they are very conspicuous, like the Iowa Memorial Union, I think they are boring. And some were left out because of geography. I have stayed within the city limits even though tempted to trespass beyond them. There is for example one house I like very much, a Spanish-Style house that was ordered by mail in the 1920s. "Spanish" meant a plain, ordinary, small, square house covered with yellow stucco and provided with a little round gable, as a sort of frontispiece, looking a little (very little) like the Alamo, although Sears Roebuck grandly named its design "The Alhambra." Unfortunately that house is an ornament not of Iowa City but of Coralville, and so it does not appear in this book.

I have been much aided. I must thank, first of all, my colleague, Robert Dykstra, Professor of History at the University, who has spent long hours expanding, and correcting, my insufficient knowledge of the history of Iowa and has helped in a thousand other ways with his inexhaustible interest, his immense erudition, and his incredible good will. I owe much to Dr. Margaret Keyes, who first suggested the idea of this book to me and whose own Nineteenth Century Home Architecture of Iowa City (University of Iowa Press, 1966) has been a source not only of indispensable information but of inspiration as well; to the State Historical Society of Iowa, whose staff and officers have been most generous and encouraging; and to Mr. Frank Seiberling, Jr. and Mr. Christopher Allen, two most gifted photographic artists, who made the most of my photographs by their skill at printing them. And finally I must give special acknowledgment to Mr. Osbert Lancaster, creator of Here of All Places and many other books, the brilliance of whose wit and style, unsurpassed, is equaled only by his distinction as a scholar of architectural history, as a social critic, and as an artist. I have borrowed from him the term and notion of the "Basic American House," and there is much else that I owe to his work.

LL
Iowa City, 1975

Contents

DORIC   IONIC   CORINTHIAN

Columns. The Greeks, over the course of 1000 years or so before Christ, gradually developed incredible engineering and mathematical skills; and either they understood beauty better than anyone before or since, or they impressed their notion of beauty, like their notion of virtue, so deeply on their heirs that it became and remained an ideal in the Roman Empire, in Christian Europe, and later in America. The ideal survived for 1000 years in the Christian era, languished, was reborn with new vitality in the fifteenth century, spread, evolved, and survived for another 500 years. In the 1930s, houses, banks, churches, schools, and gas stations were still being built in the United States in modified Greek style, in forms called Colonial or Georgian.

The Greeks had to depend on columns to hold up heavy stone roofs, the arch not yet having been invented. They converted practical necessities into artistic masterpieces, and the columns were their most conspicuous architectural legacy. Three designs evolved: Doric, Ionic, and Corinthian columns, which differed in shape and, especially, in the design of the head or "capital." The Doric was the earliest, simplest, and most dignified of the three. Ever since the fifth century B.C., Doric columns have been symbols of the perfections of classical art and of the civic spirit of the Athenian democracy. Logically, they were chosen for the Capitol of Iowa, and they supported the porches of many private houses as well. This example comes from the handsome house at 109 East Market Street, probably built in the 1850s and long the residence of Eugene Gilmore, President of The University of Iowa from 1934 to 1940.

Having created the Doric column the Greeks then yielded to what is apparently a universal impulse, to deceive the world in ornament. The second of the Greek "orders," the Ionic, did so by covering the union of the shaft and the flat piece above it (which held up the lintels of the roof) with a stone scroll. The last and showiest of the orders was the Corinthian (Corinth was a city notorious for vice and self-indulgence), which had slimmer and more elegant shafts and elaborate capitals of carved acanthus leaves. The Ionic column is from a house at 503 Melrose Avenue; the Corinthian is at 606 South Johnson Street.

I.

Ancestors

Iowa City is a classic American town. It lies a few hundred miles from the midway point between the coasts, and it was founded almost midway in time between the beginnings of national awareness in the settlements along the Atlantic and the present day. It is in a state whose population, area, and wealth are near the median of the 50 states. Its history is the history of the founding of American towns and of the American nation.

We are setting out now on a tour, a tour through time and space. Any town—and any street or building, for the matter of that—is a marvelously complicated thing made up of hidden pasts, of long forgotten causes and effects. Buildings tell stories to those who can read them, and some of the stories are very long indeed. Architecture makes lasting monuments. It is the most durable of the arts, and it is also the most inclusive. A single dwelling may instruct us in the history of mankind: in the glories and sometimes the depravities of past generations; in discoveries of engineers and chemists; in sociology and economics and taste; in the genius and folly of nations and individuals. For a building not only shelters people, it also embodies their needs and their ideas. Notions of virtue and beauty are recorded in timber, steel, and brick, and they can tell us what people have thought and done and what gods they have worshiped.

Taken together, the structures of a town reveal its personality, as a face does an individual's. Both buildings and faces are inherited, and American towns are all family albums of America's past—and of a past much older than America's. The houses and streets have family resemblances that show their descent and identify their forebears. Iowa City is a

classic example of such family traits. Its history repeats, with odd precision, the history of Philadelphia, the model and archetype of American towns. Its site and name were decided in Burlington by men who had never seen the place where it would be built, as Philadelphia had been planned and "named before it was born" by William Penn in London, in 1681. By the terms of Penn's land grant from King Charles II, "a quantity of land or ground plat should be laid out for a large town or city in the most convenient place upon the river for health and navigation." The same words might well have been used by the men at Burlington, the Legislators and the Governor of the Territory who was, by appropriate coincidence, a descendant of William Penn.

Iowa City, like its ancestor, was intended to be the capital of a new province, and its plan followed with great fidelity the model that Penn had decreed for the "greene countrie town." The network of straight streets enclosing squares, some of them left open for markets or places of wholesome recreation, reflected Penn's notions of what a healthful and convenient city should be, open and logical, in contrast to the jumbled cities of England or the older American places like Boston—whose street map, it has been said, looks like a plate of spaghetti. His notion proved popular as well as logical. It determined how American townspeople would live thereafter, from Philadelphia to San Francisco.

Many other places in North America were planned as capitals of new provinces on new frontiers. For most of them their makers conceived grand projects for public buildings and broad avenues. Sometimes enthusiasm and funds ran out, as they did in Iowa City, and sometimes the seat of government was moved, as Iowa's was when the westering flow of settlers led Iowans to choose a more central capital, as it had led Pennsylvanians to do long before.

The genesis of the American towns, however, was far older than William Penn, and its antiquity justifies the word classic in another sense. The men who designed the early America were scholars. The plan of Penn's town had itself had models consciously imitated—a long line of ancestors, Spanish-American towns, medieval garrisons, and the camps and colonies of ancient Rome. Rome's settlements, like those of North America, were built on wild and rapidly moving frontiers, and some of them, too, were the provincial capitals of empire. The Romans were imitating a still older tradition of city-making, and it befits a tradition that goes back to

The Bethel African Methodist Episcopal Church (above), at 411 South Governor Street, was built in 1868. In a predominantly white neighborhood, the plain frame building has survived in dignity as a tribute to the devotion of its congregation through more than a century.

Periclean Athens and beyond that the Capitol of the Territory of Iowa should have been provided with Doric columns that are nearly replicas of those of the Parthenon. The Americans practiced a rigorous adherence to classical architectural rules, and their public buildings, from Boston to Sacramento, recall the hope of reproducing the civic perfections of Athens in their wilderness. Iowa City is not the less American that its model was Roman and its inspiration Greek. So were the nation's.

The inhabitants of ancient Rome were cosmopolitan folk who rubbed shoulders with fellow-residents of the most varied national and religious backgrounds, as were the people of Penn's tolerant province. In the early Iowa City strange languages were heard on the streets, as they are today in the cosmopolitan university town. Varied sects built temples to God, and within three blocks of the Old Capitol there are Catholic, Methodist, Congregational, Lutheran, Unitarian, and Presbyterian churches, and Jewish and Anglican student centers. Nothing like it has ever existed in modern times outside of North America. Americans take the staggering diversity for granted, often unaware of how remarkable it is, or of how splendid its churchly monuments are, or how startling to foreign visitors. And the diversity of religions is matched by a diversity of national backgrounds not less striking. There are four Catholic churches in Iowa City: Saint Mary's was the parish church of Germans; Saint Patrick's of Irish; Saint Wenceslaus' of Czechs; and Saint Thomas More, appropriately dedicated to a scholar and housed in a building of extreme contemporary design, is the parish church of the intellectuals.

Neighborhoods separated by religion, income, or national origin are less noticeable in Midwestern towns than in the cities of the East; the outward appearance conveys architectural and sociological harmony and a mingling of income levels. There is certainly nothing visible in Iowa City to

Looking east along Jefferson Street from the Pentacrest (right). The central campus of The University of Iowa is named from its situation on the ridge above the left bank of the river occupied by five buildings—the Old Capitol and four large academic halls. It was originally the Capitol Square, the Iowa City version of that customary, indeed almost compulsory, feature of American town and city, a central open space that would be the focus of town life, reminiscent of the plazas of Spanish colonial towns.

This view from the Pentacrest shows the importance, even the intrusiveness, of the religious diversity that is a unique quality of American towns. Within sight are Saint Mary's Catholic Church and the First Methodist Church, with the beautiful Congregationalist Church and its delicate spire, built in 1868, in the foreground.

Saint Patrick's Catholic Church (above), Court Street at Linn Street, was built in 1878. Here imagination and sureness of architectural touch faltered. Although the shapes are Gothic, the suggestion of the human spirit soaring to celestial spheres is notably absent. The rose window is handsome, but the effect of the broad facade and the low belfry is one of thick-waistedness.

Saint Mary's Catholic Church (right), Linn Street and Jefferson, was finished in 1869. The parish was organized in 1840, the first in the city, and land was granted to it by the Territorial Legislature. Saint Mary's is very handsome indeed, a suitably regal tribute to the Queen of Heaven to whom it is dedicated. It is built of brick with heavily capped round-headed windows, doors, and arches in the Romanesque style that dominated church architecture beginning in what are called the Dark Ages. But in its slender, vertical shapes and its flavor of celestial aspiration, Saint Mary's belongs not at all to the Romanesque, which was somber, ponderous, and bulky; it belongs rather to the succeeding medieval style, the Gothic, which was soaring. The spire is glorious, symbolizing the skyward pointing aspiration and faith of humankind, hopeful and confident.

Saint Wenceslaus (above), East Davenport at Dodge Street, built in 1893. Like Saint Mary's and Saint Patrick's, the Catholic parish church of Saint Wenceslaus is of brick. It has a good deal of charm. The pointedness of the narrow, Gothic windows, repeated in the points of the octagonal belfry, contrast nicely with the compact body of the church and give it something of the stunning sense of community between heaven and earth that Saint Mary's spire so splendidly supplies.

Saint Thomas More, on North Riverside Drive near Park Street. Built in 1962, Saint Thomas is dedicated to the martyr-scholar who was beheaded in 1535 by Henry VIII, after serving as his Lord Chancellor, for refusing to acknowledge under oath that the sovereign was the supreme governor of the Christian Church in England. He was one of the great writers and thinkers of his time, witty, urbane, a leader of the new humanist learning of the Renaissance. "A man for all seasons," the sponsor and friend of new ideas, he is appropriately commemorated in a building that is one of the most extreme and successful examples of Modern Architecture in the city. It imitates no past and aspires to no "style." Its visual impact is entirely the product of the shapes and textures of reinforced concrete and the clever adjustment of the building to the contour of the land.

Goosetown gardens.

suggest segregation into what the Italians of centuries past called a *borghetto*—a burglet—from which our infamous ghettos sociologically and philologically descend. But beneath the rather bland harmonies of outward aspect something like *borghetti* once existed. To the northeast of Saint Wenceslaus' lay the Czech—"Bohemian"—quarter of Iowa City, and since Bohemians, often poor and markedly alien, were sometimes regarded by other settlers with disdain, their quarter was something of a ghetto. It was called Goosetown, and Goosetown today, although it has lost some of its national character, is still largely a place of houses that are faithful but small replicas of the grander houses of richer and more dominant folk. From the streets, nothing except this rather appealing quality of a town in miniature now recalls the past of Goosetown; but from the alleys a quite remarkable reminder of the past survives. It is a place of small houses but large gardens; and with their scrupulously tidy beds of vegetables, their ubiquitous vineyards, their very abundance, they bring to the Goosetown alleys the pleasant, haunting memory of a village lane in Europe.

In early America the classical tradition and the accommodation of religious and national diversity alike dictated popular education, to harmonize the emigrant traditions in a transcendent national culture, to feed the insatiable hunger for learning, and to meet the requirements of a population that not only needed but *liked* technical skills. The Americans' ingenuity and enthusiasm in matters of engineering and gadgetry surpassed even the Romans', as their enthusiasm for democracy and the liberal arts surpassed even the Greeks'.

Respect for the academies of Athens was great, and when Thomas Jefferson founded the University of Virginia, he designed a Pantheon with classical colonnades for it; esteem for *agora* and *stoa* went so far as to lead the Ohioans and Georgians to borrow the name of Athens for their university towns. The zeal for educating a much larger part of the population than any society had ever attempted before was a spectacular and impressive part of America's tradition, and Iowa City is a spectacular and impressive exemplar of it, with its university, the first to be founded west of the Mississippi, suitably seated around the Grecian columns of the Capitol.

Greek civic virtue combined with Roman cosmopolitanism

Close House, 538 South Gilbert Street at Bowery Street. This splendid residence is said to have cost $15,000, which, even when multiplied to take account of devaluations and inflations, seems cheap. It was built in 1874 by W. D. Close, the proprietor of a glove factory and a linseed oil works. He represented the somewhat conglomerate, burgeoning capitalism of young Iowa, and his house represents the impulse to establish a patrician class dedicated to display and cultural respectability, as well as large profits, in the decade after the Civil War.

It was later used as a fraternity house and then a county office, and it suffered grave depredations. An elaborate portico in the Italian Feeling was demolished, along with a balustraded terrace and gazebo or observatory on the roof. The elms died, and a widened street cost it part of its lawn. Its brick walls were painted white. But still it shows the power of strong design to survive drastic change; it retains a haunted majesty and the power to re-create, in the imagination of the onlooker, the time when its well-upholstered, newly-rich inhabitants might preen themselves, before marble mantels under gas-lit chandeliers, upon their superior taste and the fulfillment of their mission to bring Art and Culture to the frontier.

and practical skills neatly summarized the first stages of the American national experience. Dreams of virtue blended with dreams of riches; together they were the forces that moved frontiers. Both might be cheapened—into the stock rhetoric of politicians or a passionate dedication to machinery and profit margins—but together they produced miracles. A city born of such forces might turn out to be a Washington, or it might turn out to be a crooked land speculation. In the swamps of Florida and New Jersey can still be seen signs, askew and faded, that read "Twenty-first Avenue," and in the desert Southwest the unsuspecting are still buying lots that are miles from water, symptoms of fraud, of frantic optimism, and of romantic dreams. Nobility might become gullibility, and ingenuity crime, but the dreams of vast and virtuous metropolises in empty space have been very long-lived. Philadelphia was not the first, nor Iowa City the last, capital city that began as an idea. Across the oceans ideas are still producing capitals, in Australia, Brazil, and Pakistan.

Survival in the wilderness in fact required a combination of noble vision with the instincts of the explorer and the real estate promoter. Mingling, they were making the American character and turning the dreams into imposing facts. The men and women who founded Iowa City, adventurers, promoters, clergymen, merchants, farmers, and teachers, were tough and shrewd, and they were visionaries. Some of them were speculators; many were devout and educated people with a due regard for the life of the spirit and the life of the mind. Their churches and their university finely embodied spiritual and intellectual aspirations, as land speculation embodied the energetic search for riches. Other aspirations presently manifested themselves. The farmers and merchants were successful in their ventures, and success was translated, like religion and learning, into architectural opulence. Being instructed in the achievements of other ages and continents, they aspired to re-create the wonders of older worlds on the fields and bluffs of a new land. Romanticism and practicality were equally evident in their works. Romantically, they fondled phantoms of old, unhappy, far-off things, of kings and knights and castles; practically, they made enough money to build buildings that startlingly resurrected them on the prairie. And there was, too, a dreamy patriotism about the sudden appearance of Florentine villas and medieval chapels on the banks of the Iowa; Americans were resolved to show that the marvelous elegances of other peoples' Golden Ages could be duplicated inexpensively by American ingenuity. The impulse has been remarkably persistent, and it is worthy of respect.

In the decades after it was founded, Iowa City was

The house at 120 East Fairchild Street, commonly called the Swisher House for the prominent family that lived there for many years, is a beautifully preserved museum of later nineteenth-century taste. It was built in 1887, toward the end of a long-lived fashion for neo-Gothic architecture, which was supposed to adapt the features of medieval European churches to the needs of an American dwelling. It has almost everything practitioners of neo-Gothic thought was most medieval: a (tiny) window with a pointed arch; heavy, pointed caps over the windows; dormers with cut-off gables; a steeply pitched roof with a peculiar concavity at the eaves; bay windows of varied design (variety was judged to be very medieval); porches with elaborate woodwork; and, most conspicuous, what are called "bargeboards,"

decorative wooden pieces with a pierced pattern hanging from the edge of the roof over the gables.

All this looks weird and wonderful and very engagingly naive. But what is most interesting about the Swisher house is not weirdness and naivete, nor even its quite astonishing state of preservation; it is that beneath all this "carpenter Gothic" one sees very clearly the form of a Basic American House. Frame construction, porches, the cross-shaped plan, were uniquely and characteristically the elements of native building. The Gothic oddities (which indeed have little to do with medieval churches and are works of imagination) are icing on a home-baked cake of the plainest sort, a wedding cake for the marriage of sensible Midwestern folk.

For people in the 1920s, as in the Renaissance, Gothic windows looked like a travesty of true culture. Today they seem engaging and rather pathetic souvenirs of the efforts of simple people to be "in style," perhaps to make a modest gesture of recognition of a long-dead civilization whose richness they admired. There is not much of pretension or imitation in the simple little pointed window on a house at 830 Bowery Street; but it is a legacy from Chartres and Notre Dame de Paris.

The most famous painting of Iowa's most famous painter is Grant Wood's American Gothic, painted in 1930. The title involves a sort of historical pun, for "Gothic" had two quite distinct associations. Derived from the Goths, barbarians who overran the Roman Empire in the early Christian era, it was used by the enthusiasts for classical Greek and Roman civilizations— when classical ideas came back into style with the Renaissance in Europe in the fifteenth century—to describe the civilization of the unclassical Middle Ages. It meant, to them, a superstitious, primitive, savage, and ruthless era. But the Middle Ages came back into fashion at the end of the eighteenth century, and "Gothic," in the sense of medieval architecture, was much esteemed; it meant, then, piety and beauty and high culture. The trade-mark of Gothic was the pointed arch (as classical columns were the trade-marks of Greek design), and even very simple and humble houses, like the one Wood painted, were often decorated with a "Gothic" window. The stern, unimaginative farmer and his wife recall the associations with primitivism; the little window gives the painting its name and its irony. Grant Wood was dryly implying what another Midwesterner, Sinclair Lewis, had explosively stated ten years earlier in Main Street: the popular belief of the 1920s that provincial America was a wasteland of unenlightenment amounting to barbarism; the Gothic window is a symbol of the thinness of Americans' pretension to culture.

(Courtesy of the Art Institute of Chicago)

The house still stands, in Eldon, in Wapello County, on a road recently named American Gothic Street.

rapidly and abundantly furnished with re-creations, freely interpreted, of the monuments of other cultures. Even at their dreamiest, however, the pioneers usually remained thrifty. A taste for medieval cathedrals might appear in the form of a single pointed window in a frame house, and one example of this taste has become the trademark of the Midwestern tradition in Grant Wood's *American Gothic.*

The evocation of the past was almost always practical. When Iowa City Presbyterians wanted a Romanesque church that would recall the massive pieties of tenth-century Europe, they built it with the sensible, economical floor plan of the New England churches that had themselves been demonstrations both of Puritan sanctity and Yankee common sense. Their church turned into a sample, peculiar but in its way glorious, of something purely Midwestern. The legacies of seventeenth-century Massachusetts, of the chilling theology of John Calvin, and of the cathedrals of medieval Germany,

were all distinctly perceptible, but they in no way diminished the vigorous individuality of the building. Trinity, the church of the Episcopalians, reflects the same application of medieval ornament to a perfectly simple plan and structure. But the ornament here is itself very simple, merely an evocative sketching in of the medieval spirit. Economy is particularly noticeable; but so is imagination.

A very different effect inspired by the Middle Ages is to be found in the much later First Methodist Church. It is grandiloquent rather than suggestive; the facade is rather clumsily proportioned, the rough stone looks abrasive, the rose window seems to belong in quite a different sort of building, and the odd towers, with their gargoyles, seem too small for the massive wall below them. But it is imposing, and the triple portal is very handsome. It has the attraction of extreme unselfconsciousness. The architects, borrowing details at random from medieval churches of assorted sizes,

Trinity Episcopal Church, at College and Gilbert Streets, represents neo-Gothic in a most beguiling form. It was built in 1871, and with its frame construction, its simple plan, its "bàrn-siding," and its extreme austerity in the matter of ornament, it is purely and characteristically a sample of rural American. But it was intended to look Gothic, as the pointed windows and bell-tower and little triangular dormers show, and Gothic, the architecture of the Age of Faith, here is a little more appropriate and convincing than it was on Grant Wood's Eldon house. It makes, indeed, not only a suitable but a charming and handsome church. The Vestry that built and paid for it would no doubt have been startled to learn that today its most notable and engaging quality is its Americanness. They did their best to be exotic, but they were truer to themselves than they knew.

The First Presbyterian Church, Clinton and Market streets. It is the oldest of Iowa City churches, begun in 1856 and completed in 1865. It is threatened now with destruction. It would be a serious loss, for while it is not a major work of art it must be judged an imposing and beautiful example of the attempt to achieve, by using Romanesque details, the characteristic Romanesque atmosphere of slightly gloomy, fortress-like solidity in a simple and practical church building.

The First Methodist Church, at Jefferson and Dubuque streets.

eras, and locations, and incorporating them in a structure of quite inappropriate masonry and with a massiveness that is associated with a quite different age and school of design from any of the details, achieved a mixture that is monumental in every sense. On the other hand, the Danforth University Chapel, on the campus by the river, is truer to a tradition, and the tradition is a very different one: prim, simple, and neat, it recalls the classical past, and it looks so natural in its pleasant setting that its charm belies its modernity.

Taken together, the churches of Iowa City are more than monuments to the sects and eras that produced them or to the ingenuity of architects and the devotion of congregations; they form, too, a record of the history of Christianity and a memorial to the accuracy of the motto of the United States. *E pluribus unum*—unity in diversity—scarcely could be more emphatically commemorated.

The heritage of America and of all of western civilization is present and alive. Iowa City is an open archive of the way the country was settled, of inherited notions of beauty and virtue, of new ways to use resources, human and physical. There are houses and whole streets that recall the taste and tempo of different groups during the past four generations. In particular, there are records of the kind of society that developed, of the ways in which accumulating wealth and security showed itself. The builders of houses and churches and neighborhoods were the unknowing exemplars of the most conspicuous of the qualities of the Midwest, radical social mobility. In the nineteenth century, a short-lived gentry was being born of carpenters, millers, farmers, and railroad men, and they left dramatic records of their affluence and their hope for refinement. The buildings that are their monuments are, some of them, more than a century old. A not altogether dissimilar American experience is barely a decade old now, but its relics are already taking on the aspect of monuments to a passing, dramatic phase. The educational boom of the 1960s, producing some buildings of distinction and some of deplorable mediocrity, is as strikingly engraved on the face of the city as the abortive elegance of the 1870s and '80s—or that phase of exuberance for a more aristocratic educational expansion in the 1920s, when it was thought suitable to manufacture large university structures in the style of sixteenth-century Oxford.

Iowa City is, in short, an album of the American past, of its social and architectural history. It is as well an illustrated history of a past much older than America's. In an hour's walking through the town the visitor will pass by classical temples, Tudor cottages, English manors, and feudal castles. An extraordinary willingness to experiment, along with fre-

quent failure to understand the basic aesthetic principles of the originals and a desire to save money, assured that most of these importations were freely, sometimes wildly, modified. But modification is instructive too; its legacy gives us further signs and symptoms of the national genius, its vigor and its visions, its ingenuities and its fads.

The town is classical in other senses. It embodies, one may suppose, in a tolerably exact way, the notion of a metropolis as men might have conceived one in the seventeenth and eighteenth centuries. If the founder of Philadelphia could have imagined that city as it exists now he would certainly have been shocked. Faceless confusion, loss of individuality, imprisoning miles of urban and suburban growth with their throughways are the exact denial of all the social ethics of the pietists of the seventeenth or of the philosophers of the eighteenth century. What they contemplated was not a conurbation but a capital, a center for the cultural and commercial life of a region, for the coming together of cosmopolitan people and ideas and interests. Philadelphia—or New York or Chicago—are no longer centers for the surrounding countryside. It takes hours of frustration to reach them; they are isolated worlds. The proper functions of a capital can be performed only if it be easily accessible and built on a proper human scale; only recently did people begin to suppose that any place of fewer than a million inhabitants must by definition be a provincial backwater.

Iowa City is, one may guess, a good deal more like Periclean Athens than New York is. There are said to be more physicians per capita here than in any other city in the country; it would not be absurd to claim that there is more culture per square mile. With fewer than 50,000 people, it has a major art gallery and remarkable theater and music. It is an important shopping center, with the biggest bookstore in the state. And it has, too, the elusive quality that makes a city important, the quality of being a planet and not a satellite. Its planetary character is of course the result of the university. In the whole of the nation there are only three so large as The University of Iowa in towns so small. No longer the seat of government it was planned to be, Iowa City is still a capital.

The critic Naomi Bliven has written, "civilization . . . rests on two very fragile bases—high culture and good topsoil." It is hard to imagine any place where they might be more abundant, or more happily juxtaposed, than in Iowa City and the rich land around it.

The plan of almost all the older churches in Iowa City, however Gothic or Romanesque the appearances their architects aspired to, was similar to that of the churches and meeting houses of New England. But those churches, built in an age that deplored the Middle Ages as barbaric and admired the intellectual and aesthetic disciplines of Rome and Greece, had pagan, not Christian decoration. Generally it was thriftily and rather sketchily indicated. In the Danforth Chapel, a non-sectarian place of worship on the University campus, at the west end of Jefferson Street, the classical tradition appears in its simplest form. It was built in 1952, copied from a country church in Iowa, but it accurately suggests a very modest village church of an older world, and it has the stamp of classical civilization, third hand and much simplified. In this, it is the "classic" counterpart of the thin "Gothic" of Trinity. Both had ancestors very deep in the "race memory" of Europeans; but both belonged intensely to a new civilization.

A Roman Lion on the College of Engineering, at Washington and South Capitol streets.

II.

Making a City

The surveyors who were sent out from Burlington in 1839 to choose a site for a capital decided on a hill on the east bank of the Iowa River, a place some 70 miles northwest of Burlington, and about 30 from the nearest point on the Mississippi where the little settlement of Bloomington, today called Muscatine, had just been founded. The chosen place was judged to be both beautiful and healthful, safe from the floods of the capricious Iowa and bountifully provided with timber, stone, and pure water. The country between it and the settlements on the Mississippi, the plateaux that separated the valleys of the Cedar, the Iowa, and the Des Moines, was incomparably fertile. The surveyors knew that they were founding a capital for what would be a rich and populous land, and they chose carefully. But the history of the place was older, and it was not the history of political wisdom or profitable farming but of ancient cultures and trade routes.

One white man was already there. He is said to have been the first in the county and became notable in its later affairs. John Gilbert (so he called himself, but it is said that his real name was Prentice; the reason for the alias, if it was one, is not reported) was an agent of the Green Bay Trading Company. He had come from New York by way of Kentucky and was a remarkable linguist who could converse with Indians as well as trade with them. A contemporary said that he was "a fine scholar and an excellent business man," a combination entirely appropriate for the first citizen of Iowa City. He had built, in 1836, a hut and trading post a few miles south of the present city line, near Chief Poweshiek's Mesquakie village. A street was named for him; it is today the main south-to-north artery, and its four lanes of heavily traveled concrete also suggest a connection with the solitary pioneer: he was, above all, a man of commerce, and Gilbert Street with its scattered stores, warehouses, and filling stations is a not unsuitable tribute to him.

John Gilbert came as an advance agent of a conquering nation whose victory, consummated four years earlier in blood, had been only the latest of a series of sudden shifts of population and control. There are, near the city, relics of civilizations at least eight and perhaps eleven thousand years old. A variety of peoples had conquered and replaced their predecessors. The Iowa River was their main street, and in the shadowy centuries of pre-history, peoples had moved along it, and nations may have been born and died on its banks. In the 1830s, on the hills of the western shore opposite Poweshiek's village, according to the white men's legend anyway, women watched from what is today called Indian Lookout for their men's canoes returning from missions of the hunt or war.

The river had first been called, by the white men, the Buffalo River, an abbreviation of an Indian name which seems to have been "the water of the kneeling white buffalo calf." (Indians, who lived a more leisurely life than whites and had no maps, gave things more specific names.) The ways and reasons whereby it became the Iowa, and how the state and city acquired the name, have been the subject for endless investigation and sometimes acrimony. Someone in the nineteenth century claimed that "Iowa" meant "beautiful

Monument on Summit Street. The monument erected in 1839 where Summit Street intersects the line of East Court Street, marks the southeast corner of "Section Number 10," chosen by the surveyors, Swan, Ronalds, and Ralston, on commission from the Territorial Government at Burlington, as a site for a capital city for Iowa.

country." Although widely believed, this was entirely without foundation and may have been a form of real estate promotion. The facts are much more interesting, but they are confused. One thing appears, although surprising, certain: the name is connected with a notation on the map that Marquette and Joliet made after their voyage in 1673. The Reverend Father and the Hydrographer Royal of New France, nicely representing the spiritual and temporal concerns of the French Crown, were men of astonishing boldness, resolution, and science, but their notes were lost when a canoe turned over, and their information about the hinterlands of the Great River of the West was based on hearsay provided by Indians who spoke a strange language. Their map was impressionistic to a degree. They noted, among the names of many other conjectural Indian tribes, that of one they located on what looks like the Des Moines River, and they wrote it down as *Pahoutet*, which in English would be pronounced Pa-oo-tay. The name of Iowa is descended from that tribe, although the lineage is full of etymological bastardy.

The Indian people who in historical times were called the Iowas, and who may have lived near the headwaters of the Des Moines, seem to have called themselves the Pa-ho-ja, which evidently means Those With Dusty Noses. They were called by the alien Sioux (who were the informants of the French explorers) the A-yu-bha, which means Those Who Have Been Made Sleepy, probably a metaphor for "easygoing" or "peaceful." On later French maps, the people whom Father Marquette identified as the Pahoutet appear in two versions, vaguely located and variously spelled: in 1701, as Paoutova and Ajoureova (the -ova ending apparently meaning "people"); in 1708, as Pahoute and Aiaoves; in the 1720s, as simply Aroué; and by 1755, as Aiouez. This last form, presumably descended from A-yu-bha, became more or less standardized and was transliterated by English-speaking people as Aoway or, as it appears in an atlas of 1804, Ayoa and, in one of 1833, as Iaway. It no longer had much to do with the homeland of the Pahoutet; it was printed in large letters across the whole eastern part of what became the State of Iowa. Lieutenant Colonel Albert Lea, who explored and mapped the whole region, spelled it Ioway in his report of 1834. Following what seems to have been, already, common usage, he put it as a label for the river and the largely unexplored region southwest of Wisconsin, which in 1836 was officially established as the District of Ioway. By then the name was in common use. Having traveled a very great distance in time, space, and orthography, and having at the end lost its final vowel, it was accepted without question for the land and the river and, three years later, for the city. By then the Iowa Indians had left Iowa, and there was living in the river valley a much less sleepy, or peaceful, people.

The dominion of France lasted for almost 100 years after Marquette and Joliet's voyage. That of Spain, which succeeded it in 1762, lasted almost 40. French settlements flourished in the eighteenth century at Fort Chartres and Saint Louis and along the banks of the Wabash, and until the British took the Wisconsin country there was a French fort on the upper Mississippi at the place Father Hennepin had named, in 1680, Prairie du Chien. But there were few if any Europeans permanently settled in what is now Iowa until the 1790s, when Julien Dubuque started his lead mining and the Spanish government began to issue land grants. At the turn of the century Spain transferred the Louisiana country back to the French, and then, on the ninth of March in 1804, the tricolor of France was run down in the town square of Saint Louis, the flag of the United States of America was raised, and it could be proclaimed that the Mississippi ran between American shores from its source to the Gulf of Mexico.

The tricolor flies again over Iowa as its state flag. But, outside of the city of Dubuque and a dozen place-names, it is almost the only reminder of European rule, and for a generation after 1804 the American dominion remained largely titular. Iowa was Indian country for another 30 years; then it became in complicated ways a prize of war.

Most of the Indians who lived then—as they live now— in southeastern Iowa were Mesquakies, whom the white men called the Foxes. There were, however, also some Sauks or Sacs, a related but separate people. One of the Sauk leaders was a prophetic and determined warrior named Black Hawk. He had vigorously protested the establishment of Fort Madison, the first American intrusion into Iowa, in what he claimed was his people's territory. Later he resisted the whites' encroachments toward the Sauk settlement at Rock Island, on the Illinois side, although the Illinois hunting lands had been formally ceded to them. Through the summer of 1832 there were raids and battles along the Rock and the Wisconsin, and in a climactic massacre on the Bad Axe in August Black Hawk's people were driven back into the Mississippi. Sioux were lying in wait for them on the western shore, and there was more slaughter. Winnebagoes, to whom he had surrendered, turned Black Hawk over to the United States Army, and on the farm of George Davenport, a white man who was an adopted member of the Mesquakie nation, Black Hawk and the Sauk chieftain Keokuk agreed to give up their lands on the west bank of the Mississippi.

The Black Hawk Purchase opened a wide strip on the west bank to white settlers, and more was ceded by a treaty in 1836. In 1837, at the insistence of American fur traders who feared an Indian tribal war, delegates of the Mesquakies and the Sauks were summoned to Washington, and there they sold the government a million and a half acres, including the valley of the lower Iowa. The price, in cash and goods, was on the order of $375,000. Among the chiefs who signed were Keokuk, Wapello, Appanoose, and Poweshiek, and to the price they were paid may perhaps be added the honor of four Iowa counties named for them.

By then there was already a string of white villages along the Mississippi below Dubuque, and the white flood had begun to flow inland across the rich land. The counties of Dubuque and Des Moines had been organized. On July 4, 1836, the Congress had made the District of Iowa part of the new Territory of Wisconsin, and Wisconsin's first seat of government was established in Des Moines County, at Burlington, which had been laid out and named for the town in Vermont in 1834. Two years later, again on Independence Day, the Territory of Iowa was proclaimed. Robert Lucas of Virginia, the descendant of William Penn, was appointed Governor; elections were held; on the first day of November in 1838 the Assembly met, and a second government was born at Burlington.

The first concern of the Territorial authorities was to make a polity for the people, and this meant setting up counties to provide sheriffs, courts, and tax collectors. Sixteen had been hastily organized before the first legislature of Iowa met. They were given names that commemorated national and local worthies — Washington, Jackson, Van Buren, and Louisa (the last honoring a popular local heroine who had shot a man she believed had killed her father). One was named for Richard Mentor Johnson of Kentucky, who held the distinction of being the only Vice-President of the United States elected by the Senate after the Electoral College had failed to agree on a candidate. He had other distinctions too. In his earlier career he had won fame as an extreme political radical and religious skeptic, a friend of the worker and the debtor. As Vice-President he won notoriety for undignified money-grubbing, to the point of personally superintending the sale of watermelons in the inn he ran, and for moral laxity involving a *ménage à trois* with a teen-aged third wife and a black concubine.

In September 1838, Governor Lucas granted a sheriff's commission to Samuel Trowbridge to organize the government of Johnson County, and he, with the county commissioners he named, summoned a grand jury and held the first court in John Gilbert's trading post. They then set forth to lay out a county seat and build a courthouse, on the river a

The most important topographical facts of Iowa City, and the ones that decided its location, are the river and its hilly shores safe from floods and mosquitos. On the west, or right, bank of the river there are bluffs, and stone for the city was quarried from them. One quarry, on North Riverside Drive, has become a pleasant water garden.

mile or two north, and called it Napoleon.

The name was interesting: for all their democracy the pioneers liked heroes; they were, oddly, respecters of persons.* It was illuminating, and so was the indiscriminate choice of persons to respect, as exemplified in a tough frontiersman, the most drastically egalitarian of Jacksonian Democrats, and a French army officer who had flamboyantly tried to rebuild the Roman empire and appropriate the glory of the caesars. But there was an inadvertent logic as well: the imperial vision, the romantic dreams, the classical obsession, and the shrewd democracy of an inn-keeper who counted his own watermelons, were fusing into a new culture. Napoleon and its courthouse had a short life, but the fusion survived.

The town of Napoleon died and is buried by an automobile graveyard on the Sand Road, at the southern edge of Iowa City. Its demise was the work of three men named Robert Ralston, John Ronalds, and Chauncey Swan—their

The French Emperor seems to have been on the minds of early Iowans, perhaps because he was responsible for the Louisiana Purchase and thus for making Iowa possible. A hundred miles south of Napoleon, in Van Buren County, there is a hamlet called Bonaparte, and two other places were named, with fine impartiality, Marengo, after one of his most brilliant victories, and Waterloo, the scene of his final defeat.

names survive today attached to a creek, a street, and a parking plaza. In 1839, the first Legislature, sitting in the Old Zion Methodist Church in Burlington, commissioned them to select a site in Johnson County for the Territorial capital. It was voted, on January 5, that when the site was chosen it should be named Iowa City. On May 4, Chauncey Swan drove a stake into the ground on the high hill above the Iowa River where the surveyors had decided the Capitol should be built. The Legislature agreed, the Congress of the United States appropriated $20,000 for a building to house the government, and Iowa City was born.

The hilltop where Chauncey Swan drove his stake, on the date that is now celebrated as Founder's Day, was a mile or more north of Napoleon, on the east bank, a little upstream from the place where the river flows out of a narrow, twisting valley between steep hills in the highland into wide, rich bottomland called, then and now, Pleasant Valley. The site commanded a broad view up and down the river and of the bluffs across it. It was densely covered with bur oak and hazel, and the work of clearing it commenced at once. By the Fourth of July, 1839, Independence Day for both the United States and the Territory, it was far enough advanced that a large picnic could be held on the site to celebrate the birth of a new capital city.

Upriver from the Park Street Bridge, the Iowa flows between wooded hills on the east bank and the City Park on the west. Here it is possible to re-capture something of the appearance that the scene must have had when Iowa City was founded. The little house in the distance was built in the 1850s. It was on the stagecoach road to the west and once was an inn. A tunnel between its cellar and a cave in the back yard gave rise to the story that it was a station on the underground railway.

It was a strange picnic. There were no roads. Visitors came on horseback, and provisions came by wagon over new and crudely cut trails. The food for the festivity was cooked in the kitchen of one Jonathan Harris, who lived four miles away to the south. But the new Iowans, intensely and self-consciously dedicated to symbols, were also sufficiently bold and vigorous to overcome obstacles. Their vigor was, in fact, incredible, and so was the speed with which they worked. The work of laying out the town went very fast. By August, lots were being offered for sale, and a general store was doing business in the first frame building to be built, on Clinton Street facing the Capitol site, which is still the center of the shopping district. A lawyer, a physician, and a minister of the gospel were in residence. A block house had been built at the corner of Iowa Avenue and Dubuque Street, and a sawmill established (it could not supply the demand, and lumber was brought from Kentucky and Ohio by water to Muscatine, whence it was laboriously dragged to Iowa City). In September 1839, Chauncey Swan opened an inn.

It was a sort of instant city; the population, it seemed, was appearing spontaneously. A post office was established. Lots were sold at auction, some of them to eastern real estate speculators. Streets, still mostly conjectural, were appearing along the lines laid down in a plan drawn up before the site had been finally decided on. They followed rigorously William Penn's plan, with amendments inspired by the monumental and patriotic model of Washington. Like the counties, they would be given the names of the great men of the nation—Washington, Jefferson, Madison, Van Buren, and

Johnson (it is interesting that neither of the Adamses was honored)—and of the great men of nascent Iowa—Lucas, Dodge, and Gilbert—or of the Iowa towns that already existed—Dubuque, Bloomington, Clinton, Davenport, and Burlington, forming a tolerably complete gazetteer of the Iowa of 1839. There was one boulevard which, like Pennsylvania Avenue, was to run between the Capitol and the Executive Mansion. It was named Iowa Avenue; at the site for the Capitol it intersected Capitol Street, at the site of the Executive Mansion, Governor Street. There were to be (as in Philadelphia) five open squares. The whole conception was very philosophical; it bespoke a rationalism that did not entirely connect with the realities of topography or the needs of even horse-drawn traffic. But it was a conception that by then was taken by town builders as an imperative; it was the very pattern of America, as the no less rigid section lines of the countryside were the very pattern of the Midwest.

The town grew with prodigious speed as adventurous settlers and speculators streamed in. They came by water, or by horseback across the prairie, or down the old path, newly marked by a ploughed furrow, on the line of the present highway from Dubuque and Prairie du Chien. Farmers, artisans, shopkeepers, and politicians appeared. They first built cabins, of logs and puncheons and shakes, and then houses of the yellow stone that was being quarried from the hills by the river—five of the old stone houses survive—or of bricks from Sylvanus Johnson's newly opened brickyard on the river. A year after its founding, Robert Lucas rode with his daughters from Burlington to inspect a raw but considerable village, with a population that had reached 700.

Most of the earliest houses were log cabins or shed-like frame structures with rough shingle siding. But stone, the local yellow sandstone (which was judged more durable than the white limestone of the Old Capitol), was also used. The little house at 614 North Johnson Street (above left) shows what many of the early stone houses must have looked like. In 1846, it was owned by Almon Barnes and was probably built by him then or a little earlier. It is a rectangle of the simplest sort, and it looks much like farmhouses in older parts of the country, wherever there was native building stone to be found. The transom-light was a feature of old Colonial houses, but the very low-pitched roof is novel; in the East the early houses generally had steep roofs with gables that formed right triangles, permitting the use of the top story for bedrooms or attic space. The low-pitched roofs in Iowa, which sacrifice space that could have been added at little extra cost or labor, may reflect the hazards of high winds.

Three other stone houses (another, considerably altered and not shown here, survives at 332 South Governor Street) show evolving standards of comfort and refinement. In one, at 410 East Market Street (directly above), considerable attention was paid to appearances; people were beginning to seek beauty as well as shelter, as the classical attachment to symmetry, balance, and sound proportion shows. It was built in the late 1840s or early 1850s by Henry Nicking. The second, at 119 Park Road (overleaf above) similarly symmetrical and carefully proportioned, was a farmhouse, originally outside the city, probably built by one Robert Hutchinson, who received the land from the Territory in 1843. The house was built soon after. The half dormers are recent additions, and it once had a lower roof-pitch and a front porch, but the basic design keeps the solid, formal dignity of the original. The third house, at 219 North Gilbert Street (overleaf below), was built a few years later. It is larger and more imposing. Its fine form and woodwork are very much in the classical tradition of the elaborate Colonial houses of the East; it might be anywhere in New York or Pennsylvania except for the color and the texture of the stone, which is characteristically local.

It is said that there was only one dwelling in the place that afforded suitable lodging for the gubernatorial ladies, but there were plenty of buildings for lesser personages. And, on Independence Day of 1840, the cornerstone of the great stone Capitol was laid.

The construction, like that of so many American public buildings, was beset with difficulties, delays, and charges of incompetence and corruption. Costs were, as they usually are, drastically underestimated. Builders and superintendents, including Chauncey Swan, were denounced and dismissed. Impatient, the government moved from Burlington, and the Legislature convened for the first time in Iowa City in December 1841, but it was obliged to meet for many months in an inconvenient frame house. It moved into the Capitol long before the building was finished. In its stately chambers Iowa was made and statehood proclaimed in 1846. But there was still work to be done in 1857 when Iowa City lost its temporal dignity and the government moved again, to Des Moines. By then, though, for all the delays and complaints, the Capitol, standing much as it stands today, was magnificent. The proportions are very true. Even now, when it is dwarfed by the oversized neo-classical academic halls around it, it is enormously impressive, and it looks far larger than it is. From the river side it rises with incomparable majesty, enthroned above the water on its steep and verdant hillside.

The contrast between its splendor and the raw town that was growing around it in the 1840s must have been strong, the contrast between the two sides of the American character. On the one hand was the Jeffersonian idealism of democrats, learned in the classics, dreaming of a new Athens, building to demonstrate the dignity of the state and its citizens, achieving imposing massiveness and serenity. On the other was the daring of the adventurous explorers, vigorous and shrewd, imaginatively seeking out the chance to turn a quick dollar, the friendly, neighborly, proudly self-sufficient individualists, promoters, pioneers, jerry-builders brave and careless. The new town smelled strongly of their rowdiness and profiteering. In 1857, Horace Greeley reported to the readers of the *New York Tribune* that in Iowa City "almost everyone who isn't drunk is getting rich."

The Capitol on its square was noble and beautiful, but it stood for what was often noticeable in America, a feeling that beauty and dignity and tradition had little to do with ordinary life. It was a tension of opposites that made the nation and sent the pioneers onward, ravaging, building, and dreaming dreams as they went, across the wide Missouri to the mountains and the western coast.

The east front of the Old Capitol, the chief architectural and historical glory of Iowa City, and of the state. It must rank as one of the handsomest nineteenth-century public buildings in the classic style in the United States.

In the sculpture that prolifically adorned their temples the Greeks depicted native deities and flora and fauna. At the time of the birth of the new American Republic, it seemed a good idea to glorify the new nation in its own classical age by using American flora and fauna (on public buildings deities were avoided as violating the First Amendment of the Constitution). Ears of corn and other American vegetation appeared on the Capitol at Washington. In Iowa City, when the great classical university buildings were designed for the Pentacrest at the end of the nineteenth and the beginning of the twentieth centuries, they were enlivened with stone turkeys, eagles, bison, sheep, and squirrels, and, in a blind arch over the door of Schaeffer Hall, an anonymous Indian chief. The sculpture on Schaeffer and Macbride Halls is entertaining and imaginative. Probably not more than one passerby in a hundred looks up to enjoy it.

III.

The City as a Museum

The varied and sometimes clashing traits of the frontier settlement, the American Synthesis, persisted. Diverse backgrounds blended in what was not so much, perhaps, a melting pot as a sort of mulligan stew with its own definite flavor but with each component separate and identifiable. The people of Iowa City remained diverse, dynamic and romantic, visionary and practical, avaricious and generous, rough and refined, and all this opulent confusion was written into their town.

The aspiration to high ideals, to reviving great and ancient virtues, was supremely manifested in the classic Capitol, and its themes were repeated as the town grew with startling speed from sprawling adolescence to adulthood as a capital. Greek columns multiplied on porches, pilasters, and porticos, symbols of the endless vitality of the ideals of Athens. On a newly civilized frontier, the business of the new ladies and gentlemen was to reproduce as quickly as possible the outward signs of what had meant, for 3000 years, civilization. Most of the pioneers had no aspiration to build a different one.

Later, farther west, they would do so, constructing the world of sheriff and saloon, of range and rustler, a native civilization that still has power to stir imaginations on the screen of every television set in the world. The magnetism of the Old West proved very lasting, but its roots were shallow; the older tradition replaced it when the economy of the plains and mountains changed. In Iowa, the economy was from the beginning a familiar one; the crops and the landscapes were like those the settlers knew, and lent themselves to an imported social order. In the end, the Midwest would produce its own civilization, more lasting than that of the Far West, but at the beginning the idea was to improve an old civilization. By 1850, a settled society with hints of hierarchy and luxury was emerging in an old pattern. The 5000 people then in Iowa City were for the most part native-born Americans. The immigrants were beginning to come, but most of the citizens had been born in Indiana, Ohio, or Pennsylvania. They were reliving the east-coast experience in a speeded-up progression from log cabin to stately home.

The progression is queerly illustrated in one surviving stately home which *contains* the only surviving log cabin. It was part of Rose Hill, the property of Captain Frederick Macy Irish, an early and apparently a rather rowdy settler. He had been tried for his part in a lynch-murder and had once been prosecuted for selling whiskey to the Indians. But, like so many others, he became a man of substance, a founder of the Iowa Union Railroad and of the *Press*, which is still Iowa City's daily paper. In 1898, his reminiscences of the old days were published in the *Annals of Iowa* and furnished ample evidence of the transition from frontier to decorum. He wrote, "the natives were generally well-disposed toward their white neighbors, and save when under the influence of whiskey seldom gave trouble." This lofty tone had its counterpart in the history of his log cabin, first built in 1840. In 1870, after Irish had sold it, it was surrounded by an elegant villa in the French Taste, with features borrowed from plantation houses in Virginia. It had a mansard roof, a cupola, and two-story porches (which were in a Taste not at

In a society that relied on the horse for all local transport it was necessary to provide watering troughs, mounting blocks, and hitching posts along the curbs. (It was also, of course, necessary to provide commodious stables, expensive carriages, and an army of workers to clean the streets; it is easy to forget how dirty and inconvenient horse-drawn traffic was, and how expensive.) At least one mounting block survives (above), on Summit Street, along with three hitching posts; this one at left is in the 600 block of East College Street.

Rose Hill. Captain Irish's log cabin (from which he moved to a handsome brick house nearby about 1850) was transformed into an elaborate mansarded manor house by William Hamilton, late of Mount Vernon, Iowa. Its little tower and its mansard were later removed and replaced with a "hip" roof, and the house has been repainted in accordance with the "Colonial" taste of the twentieth century, which demanded white. The original columns and the characteristic railing of the second story porch, suggestive of a southern plantation house, survive. The house is at 1310 Cedar Street.

Plum Grove. The beautiful house of Robert Lucas, Iowa's first Territorial Governor, was built in 1844. Along with its pleasant grounds it was restored in 1946. The exterior is very plain, almost bare, but the proportions are admirable. It represents, better than anything else in Iowa City, a great American tradition inherited from England, whither, in turn, it had come originally from the ancient world via Renaissance Italy and seventeenth-century Holland. Red brick, light-colored wood, multi-paned windows, forth-right moldings and eaves, and simple dignity were the hall-marks of great houses in Philadelphia, Williamsburg, and Boston. Plum Grove, which is open to the public, is at the end of Carroll Street, a dead end off Kirkwood Avenue.

all French but rather Old South). Having lost its mansard (but not its porches) it still stands on its hilltop in extensive grounds, on what is now Cedar Street, the nearest thing to a manor that Iowa City can show.

A log cabin enclosed in a manor house in the French Taste (with Southern porches) showed what happened when pioneers made money. And money oozed from the surface of the prairies. Soon, with the railroads, it became a flood, and a shell of refinement was rapidly constructed around the log cabin society. Cyrus Clay Carpenter, coming from Pennsylvania to seek his fortune on the frontier, reached Iowa City in the spring of 1854. He was displeased by the smell of profits that was a symptom of the railroad fever. The capital, he wrote, was "assuming a good many airs," and he traveled on, to the little outpost at Fort Dodge where he would make a home and a career that took him to the governorship.

Behind the frontier new opulence required a more elaborate setting than the native architectural tradition could provide. What had been elegance enough for Robert Lucas in his fine, classically simple residence at Plum Grove would by the 1860s look uncouth to the newly rich. Something much more conspicuous in the way of elegance was required, and if it could combine the symptoms of such diverse aristocracies as those of Bourbon France and Virginia planters, so much the better.

In the early years there were nonetheless handsome houses in the Greek tradition, with columned doorways that faithfully reproduced the three "orders" of classical architecture, Doric, Ionic, and Corinthian, as shown on page eight. The taste for them long persisted; they were still being built in the 1880s. But most of the classical legacy was gradually forgotten; the dignified simplicity of Plum Grove was submerged in a rising tide of ornament. Oddly, one detail triumphantly rode across the high seas of Victorian taste into the more tranquil waters of the Greek Revival at the end of the century: the oculus, or bullseye window in the gable end, appeared in dozens of unexpected places, in an elegant Italian villa of the 1880s, then, during the Greek Revival, in the large temple-like edifice that was judged suitable to house a College of Engineering, and in a stiff neo-Georgian house of the 1920s. By that time it had become fashionable to imitate America's own architectural past.

Oculi. Little round windows in gable ends continued in vogue until the 1940s, demonstrating a remarkable continuity of taste. From the house at 829 Kirkwood Avenue, built in the 1870s; the College of Engineering at the southwest corner of Washington and South Capitol Streets, built in 1905; and the Baptist Student Center, at 230 North Clinton Street, built in the 1920s.

In the meanwhile, however, it had been fashionable to imitate everyone else's. Opulence frequently breeds a contempt for what is native, and in the later nineteenth century Gothic, Italian, French, Swiss, Moorish, and even Egyptian "styles" baroquely burgeoned. And this architectural ecstasy undoubtedly reflected a very un-native readiness to imitate

The house above, at 829 Kirkwood Avenue, illustrates the transition from America's Georgian colonial tradition, so handsomely embodied in Plum Grove, to the Victorian idea of "richness" that supplanted it. It was built in the 1870s, a generation later than Plum Grove. The basic forms are similar, with the red brick and gables, but elaboration and distortion is already well-advanced. The height of ceilings, and accordingly of outside walls, has begun to rise. Heavy lintels have appeared. Bracketing—still quite modest—has appeared on the eaves. A veranda and bay windows have been added. The floorplan has become more complicated. Symmetry has been abandoned. The determinants of the first stage of the Victorian house are all there, although in rudimentary and dignified form.

Twenty years later, when the house opposite was built, the Victorian elements had obscured the Georgian tradition. What began as fanciful amendment with modest borrowings from other styles and ages ended up in an orgy of meaningless mixtures of alien tastes, and the classical tradition was, for a time, lost. It would be reborn shortly after the second house was built, perhaps as a reaction to the excesses of indiscipline it represents.

Old-World ostentation and class distinctions; the results would have made Thomas Jefferson's hair stand on end, and in fact stalwart sons of the old frontier united with sons of the old Eastern gentry in horror at what was happening to American taste. In 1873, Mark Twain gave the era a name in *The Gilded Age*, and in 1890, William Dean Howells would point out the *Hazard of New Fortunes*. They were both transplanted Midwesterners, lamenting days of easy money and the dying republican simplicity of their boyhoods in Missouri and Ohio, although Mark Twain eventually fell victim to the taste for lavishness and built himself an extravagant and exotic villa in Hartford.

Henry Adams, who counted two presidents of the classic age among his forebears, was the epitome of what Oliver Wendell Holmes called the Boston Brahmins. He, too, conceived that American taste was being ruined by easy money. Certainly it was being changed. New fortunes were buying scrollwork for eaves and turrets for roof-tops. Benjamin Franklin Allen spent $250,000 building Terrace Hill in Des Moines. It was, and still is, the grandest house in Iowa, a towered palace in what was imagined to be the style of the French Renaissance. One day it would house the governors of Iowa; if Henry Adams could have foreseen it he would have shuddered and resumed his cloistral contemplation of the moral and aesthetic purities of Mont Saint Michel and Chartres.

What was happening had its precedents, however, much older than Henry Adams or even his great-grandfather John. The Gothic—or medieval—was one of the first of the borrowed (and heavily ornamented) styles—and it had been revived as early as the middle of the eighteenth century, in the beginning as a sort of joke in the Age of Reason, when the word Gothic was still a synonym for barbaric and superstitious. The revival flourished and ceased to be a joke. Washington Irving rebuilt his house on the Hudson to make it look Gothic. In the 1840s, a talented nurseryman named Andrew Jackson Downing was writing books about domestic architecture and commending the virtues of something called a *cottage orné*, which sounded glamorous in French but meant merely a decorated cottage, a rambling, asymmetrical, and vaguely medieval house. The laws of proportion so painstakingly worked out by the builders of the Parthenon meant nothing to him. Downing wanted a picturesque and rustic mood and sought it in steep-pitched roofs and generous amounts of carpentry, the products of power-driven lathes and jigsaws that were intended to suggest the lacy stonework of late medieval churches. He spoke to the condition of his age: fretwork began to drip from cornices and doorways.

The Gothic Revival flourished as people tired of classical restraint and formality and became beguiled by what were hazily called the Middle Ages. Gothic houses were romantically nostalgic, but until much later nobody thought to try to imitate literally the very expensive kind of masonry and stone-carving that had been the most conspicuous features of the originals. One Gothic fashion was for steep-roofed rustic "cottages," which were intended to—and indeed did—exude charm, although the Middle Ages were only very faintly perceptible. The characteristic fretwork is gone from the house below at 918 Bowery, which was built about 1870, and it is now painted Colonial yellow and white, but the charm bountifully survives. A brick dwelling (opposite below) at 704 Reno Street, built in 1870 next to the city cemetery (to which its decidedly ecclesiastical design seems suitable) is much simpler, but as well as any house in Iowa City it shows the attraction that Gothic windows had for people, and that they can give to what is really just an ordinary Basic House a characteristic twist and charm. The faintest possible gesture in the direction of the Middle Ages is to be found in the nice, angular house (opposite above) at 1106 Bloomington Street, but the "carpenter Gothic" on the gable ends is enough to give it a very strong character, too.

President Gilmore's house at 109 East Market, from which the Doric column on p. 8 was taken, illustrates the way in which alien ornament began to be added to houses in the 1850s to dress them up. Under the paint that covers its brick, the Gilmore House is very similar to Plum Grove, but it is a little more elaborate, with its wider eaves and their decorative "brackets," and its quite intricate wooden porch. This was the beginning of the Italian Style, which was believed, on very slender grounds, to suggest villas of the Renaissance landscape.

The pointed arch, in times when buildings were of stone and there was no steel or mortar, permitted a much loftier vault than the round-headed arch and had made possible the soaring naves of the great cathedrals. Now it appeared, without any structural justification at all, in the gables of little frame and brick cottages, and it became the trademark of its day—and, years later when Grant Wood worked it into his symbolic painting, of the Midwest. The Gothic windows and the *cottages ornés* were still quite simple, and the surviving examples are appealing. They were the innocent forerunners of the tidal wave that submerged Republican Simplicity.

Ornament and imitation had caught on. Then opulence produced some more changes in American houses. The most striking changes were the lofty ceilings and the corresponding increase in the height of buildings, symptoms of the neglect of the Greek law of proportions. Given the American summer there was some practical reason for high ceilings, but the enthusiasm for elongation exceeded anything practicality might have demanded. Tallness was liked for its own sake: it is interesting that artists who were drawing pictures of buildings such as Independence Hall (where the Greek proportions were strictly adhered to) drew them distortedly tall, with unnaturally elongated windows. The actual shape of Independence Hall looked, to people living a century and a half after it was built in the 1730s, *squat*.

The excesses of elongation came gradually. Ceilings rose at first by inches; later they rose by feet. As they went up, other trademarks of the Gilded Age began to appear: windows with heavy cappings and arches, either round or, more deplorably, segmental arches (the segmental arch, a flattened arch made of small segments of a semi-circle, is a difficult shape to handle; it quite often looks heavy and awkward). Bay windows, which had appeared very rarely in the past several centuries, recurred in profusion, like the petals of an opening flower. Porches (the word is merely the French for "porticos") were originally small projections providing shelter for people waiting on doorsteps, but they grew into broad verandas encircling the whole house and became a peculiarly American institution. Like high ceilings they had a good deal of justification in a hot climate (the word "veranda" came from India, which is even hotter than the United States), and they lent themselves to prodigious amounts of wooden decoration. The veranda had its aesthetic uses, too. It helped compensate for the extreme verticality of the houses. Much later, owners of Victorian verandas found them gloomy and expensive to keep up, as well as old-fashioned, and destroyed them in large numbers. They thereby wrecked the composition and proportions of their houses.

These features were copiously present in houses of the Italian Taste, which joined the Gothic in popular esteem in the 1850s. Early "Italian" houses, like the Gilmore House, were quite simple, and some still had Grecian columns and little but elaborate brackets on the eaves and verandas to indicate—however obscurely—their Italianness. Even at their plainest, though, they were clearly intended to suggest grandeur instead of rustic simplicity like that of the Gothic cottages. Generally their link with Italy is remote, often to contemporary eyes undiscoverable, but some of them have definite associations, like the little rectangular windows under wide eaves that are a feature of houses in Venetia. Most such gestures were superficial; the house, decorated and elongated, remained at core a Basic American House with the simplest sort of plan. But by the 1870s, decoration had become much more conspicuous; it had begun, indeed, to run wild.

There was authority for all this. The immensely influential English art critic, John Ruskin, was in love with Venetian palaces and with French cathedrals and the religious statuary and stone lacework with which they were frequently enveloped. He proclaimed to the world that Architecture was Ornament—everything else was mere engineering—and the world listened. (It was a mistake that would be over-corrected when the great Chicago architects, Louis Sullivan and Frank Lloyd Wright, launched the Modern Movement, which would lead to the austerity of modern skyscrapers and the creed that ornament is immoral.) Richard Morris Hunt of New

There was a rage for bay windows. (The word "rage" means a fit of either insanity or lust, but it came to be used as a slang word for "the latest thing.") One is shown here on the house at 318 Jefferson Street, built in the early 1880s in the Italian Style, which was already getting a little old-fashioned by then.

This bay window is so oddly located, amid such luxuriant wooden shrubbery, as to suggest an enormous nose protruding from a thicket. It is hard for the cynical twentieth century to avoid the suspicion that the architecture, like the morals, of people a hundred years ago was the product of a deliberate effort to be funny. But that, of course, was not the case. In both architecture and morals the Victorians were dedicated to the intensely serious business of concealing reality, in the belief that success in doing so was proof that humanity was progressing toward a higher artistic and moral state of being.

The University Institute for Public Affairs at 507 North Clinton Street. This stately house, well preserved and splendidly situated on the high bluff above the left bank of the river, is an early example of the Italian influence applied to a Basic American frame house. It was built in 1857 for Peter Dey, a railroad man and banker. He later added the wing in the original style, and except for the color of the paint and the loss of its shutters, it looks much as it must have in his lifetime. The two pairs of shutters that do survive on the south wall are fakes; there are no openings behind them. They were added to break up a blank wall, and they foreshadow the relentless dedication that was overcoming Americans to concealing realities in the interests of an artistic appearance. The prominent lintels, the porch with its triple, clustered pillars, the purely ornamental brackets under the eaves, the tentatively arched window in the gable, these too are the innocent forerunners of the dedication to a "rich effect."

1142 East Court Street. The house attracts sightseers because it was for many years the residence of Iowa's most famous painter, Grant Wood. It was built in 1850 adjacent to the first brickyard in Iowa City by the yard's owner, a man named Nicholas Oakes. Wood restored it to its present delightful and presumably original state. As with the Gilmore House, the complicated (and structurally useless) brackets on the eaves illustrate very clearly the first stages of the mania for decoration applied to a perfectly straightforward Basic American House. Its ground-floor windows show the growing taste for elongation, which led eventually to ceilings 15 feet high or more.

415 South Summit Street. The people of the countryside in northeast Italy, the mainland of Venice, have summers rather like Iowa's, and they resisted them by building square houses with thick stone walls and small windows, and very wide eaves on low-peaked, "hip" roofs for shade. The garrets were lit by little rectangular windows under the eaves. Such houses set a style in colonial America—the rich sea-captains of Salem, Massachusetts, particularly liked them and built magnificent adaptations in brick in the eighteenth century. They came back into fashion in the second half of the nineteenth, when they were much more drastically adapted, being built of wood with large plate-glass windows, porches, and fancy woodwork, and in this handsome example, a central "pavilion" with its own gable. It was built in 1879, toward the end of the fashion for the Italian Style so popular a few decades before.

York, a very successful architect, proclaimed that Americans should practice Adaptation and proved it by profitably providing the Vanderbilts with a medium-sized fifteenth-century French château on a corner lot on Fifth Avenue. Fastidious ladies, in an age when sloth was a test of female refinement, proclaimed their faith in the Artistic and spent cloistered days embroidering green velvet so that it looked like moss, which would make pincushions Artistic.

Taken together, Adornment, Adaptation, and the Artistic produced what would later be called monstrosities. Even in Iowa, where there were fortunately no Vanderbilts to finance châteaux, there were Allens to finance Terrace Hill, and Larrabees to pay for their astonishing Montauk at Clermont. Flowery excesses bloomed around the roofline, and stalactites hung from lintels and porches. There is one startling, if relatively modest, sample of the Adorned, Adapted, and Artistic Palace in Iowa City. The Gotch House, surviving in almost its original form, still purveys the flavor its builders sought, of overpowering magnificence.

Terrace Hill, Montauk, and the Gotch House sum up what Henry Adams and his like thought materialism was doing to American culture, reducing it to something showy, ill-proportioned, undisciplined, hideous, indecent. But such conceits were perhaps less lamentable than he thought. The contrast of two doorways, one orthodox and splendidly Greek, the other of a rather serpentine Baroque, need not be seen as the contrast between the true and the vulgarly false but rather between a rigid intellectual tradition and romantic originality. Contemporary critics like Henry Adams must be judged unduly suspicious of innovation and perhaps of imagination. For innovation and imagination were quite as noticeable as meaningless ornament in the years between 1870 and 1900, although it is not surprising that admirers of Monticello and Mount Vernon overlooked them. Adaptation was

The Gotch House, at 1110 East Kirkwood Avenue, shows clearly how the thirst for opulence was an addiction that required larger and larger doses. It was built for a prosperous meat-packer about 1880. A plain and sensible core—a square in this case—is covered with details, here overpoweringly dominant in contrast to the discreet intimations of imported elegance on the Dey House. There is a hip-roof with a balustraded platform or balcony on top of it. There is much noticeable decoration under the eaves. There are, almost unique on private houses in Iowa City, quoins—heavily accented stone blocks— at the corners. (Quoins were, in earlier times, structurally necessary in some stone buildings to provide stability for thin stone walls; here they are structural phonies). There is that popular feature, the bay window. There is a fancy porch. There are large round-arched windows and doors with emphatic (and structurally pointless) cappings. There is, finally, an almost total failure of any sense of proportion. Contrary to all instincts and all rules of past times, the upper story looks higher than the lower, giving an odd top-heaviness that the Victorians apparently thought imposing. All in all, the Gotch House deserves special attention, both for its curious aberrations from sound design and for the undeniable impact they produced. It may be hard for the viewer to know what reactions he is having, whether he is dazzled, amused, stunned, or horrified; but powerful reactions are certain, and calling forth powerful emotions is a sort of test of architectural achievement, one that split-levels and ranch houses will assuredly never pass.

Part of the reason that houses of the late nineteenth century looked fantastic was, no doubt, simply that they represented so large a break from the familiar traditions of architectural orthodoxy. A classic portico (above) like the Corinthian one at 606 South Johnson Street, is really quite as elaborate as the Victorians' excesses, but it represents a tradition, and a sense of proportion, so ancient and persistent as to seem right and proper. It looks, today, natural; by contrast, the remarkable doorway (right) at 9 South Linn Street is startling because it belongs to no tradition. Its parts do—the lower panels are adapted versions of the "coffered" design that ancient Romans used (mostly on their ceilings) and which was widely imitated in the Georgian Age. The glass panels are of a shape—that of curvacious teardrops—that was familiar in the Baroque Age of the seventeenth century. But putting together one tradition with another seems like a startling impropriety. The parts are old, but the whole gives the viewer the shock of the new. Bold originality is always unsettling. It is also usually a measure of both intellectual indiscipline and intellectual vitality.

The Charles Addams House, today judged an appropriate residence for monsters and phantoms, was in its day associated with the showy magnificence of the Age of Louis XIV as revived, reinterpreted, and much amended by Napoleon III, the raffish Emperor of the French, in the 1850s and 1860s. The munificent Emperor built his new Paris in marble and sandstone; thrifty Iowa City built its French houses in frame and usually kept a familiar floor-plan and some familiar features of earlier fads, like the Italian porch (above) at 506 College Street. A block away was a more opulent version (overleaf), today delightfully repainted and restored as a sorority house. The aspect and atmosphere of houses of the French Style are all their own, but they are still much the same kinds of houses, with higher ceilings and longer windows, that had been built in America for several hundred years.

mostly practiced in a form so free that, as the Italian Taste showed, its results had almost nothing to do with its inspiration.

After Italy came France, and France provided an inspiration even more hospitable to Adornment, Adaptation, and the Artistic. Several kinds of French styles were experimented with, but the most distinctive is that which reinterpreted, with a freedom verging on promiscuity, a favored device of François Mansart, who designed the royal palace of Versailles for Louis XIV. The final consonant of his name, like almost everything else about Mansart, got changed in translation. What are called mansard roofs, in their original form, permitted the addition of attics, often of several stories, without disturbing the proportions of the walls or requiring expensive masonry and buttresses. For frame or brick houses they were absolutely without structural justification.

When Paris, the mecca of all artistically sensitive people, was rebuilt by the third Napoleon in the 1860s, the mansard roof was revived, became modish, and remained so for a long time. In public buildings it was usually accompanied by a great many rococo stone pillars, wreaths, statues, and coats of arms. In ordinary dwellings such expensive features were absent or sketchily indicated in wood and cast iron. Still, the houses with the mansard roofs, often accompanied by towers with steep slate bonnets (features that would have startled François Mansart, since they derived from Italian models quite alien to his restrained designs) formed a most distinctive product of Victorian architecture. In the twentieth century, Americans would rename them after a talented cartoonist, Charles Addams, who used M. Mansart's distorted legacy as a symbol for obsolete eeriness and fantasmal menace. Obviously, gloom and menace were absent from

The Swiss Style, which had nothing much to do with Switzerland, was manifested mainly in a sort of wooden lattice-work screen hung from the peaks of gable ends. Such screens were details, but they undoubtedly did produce a special atmosphere that dramatically changed the character of a plain frame house. At 419 Summit Street, Lovell Swisher built in 1879 a stately home. Its stateliness lies chiefly in the decorative Swiss screen, which gives remark- *able distinction to what is otherwise a well-proportioned but not very interesting house. Swisher was a bookkeeper who became a leading banker. He and his stately home precisely summarize the story of accumulating wealth and artistic strivings that were making what almost became a Midwestern aristocracy.*

their original owners' notion of what they were living in. Today, when they are freshly painted and freed of the jungle with which Victorians—like present-day houseowners—injudiciously surrounded them in the belief that shrubbery will stay the same size as when it is planted, Charles Addams Houses may appear as originally conceived: handsome, stately, even cheerful.

After France, Switzerland. It is difficult to think of any kind of building less plausible in Iowa than a chalet meant for snow-topped Alps, but chalets were vastly admired. A "Swiss Chalet" meant, in nineteenth-century America, nothing more than some fanciful woodwork appended to gable ends and entranceways. It was cheap and easy to build (although costly and difficult to maintain) since it could be mass-produced and nailed into place, forming a sort of lace-

like wooden screen suspended from overhanging eaves. Where it survives, it gives to plain, forthright houses a characteristic charm.

There were also experiments with varieties of classical modes, often "adapted" from northern Italy in the sixteenth century, in the style sometimes called Palladian after its greatest exponent, Andrea Palladio. It had been adapted by Palladio from ancient Rome and readapted in the eighteenth century. Most Palladian buildings were large affairs like museums, but Palladian themes were worked into Victorian frame houses as well. Palladio-Victorian buildings had emphatic squareness with flat lintels and pillars and moldings with classical patterns, often beautified by little wooden teeth, which were reminders that several thousand years earlier the ends of joists had extended beyond the tops of

The house at 609 Summit Street shows that the Roman models could be modified to the uses of Adornment. This fine, forthright house of the earliest phase of the "Classic Revival" was built about 1895. Its porch pillars, its lintels, its moldings, its air of squareness, all contribute to what late Victorians hoped was a Roman effect.

Sometimes a more serious effort was made to capture the Roman tradition, in this case in the form in which seventeenth-century builders used it. But the nineteenth century did not sacrifice its peculiar devotion to vertical distortions and to oversized treatment of the details it tried to imitate. The portal of Calvin Hall, built in 1884 on West Jefferson Street at North Capitol, is "correct" enough in its basic forms, but they are all out of proportion, and their relation to one another produces a massive heaviness that would have outraged the rigorous precisionists of Stuart England.

walls for greater stability. Another source of inspiration was Pompeii, whose ruins were being excavated and whose horrible fate attracted the somewhat morbid imagination of the Victorians and had a huge public owing to the popularity of Edward Bulwer-Lytton's romantic novel, *The Last Days of Pompeii*. Pompeian decorative themes, like Palladian ones, were translated to Iowa in wood, in the form of cheap but charming machine-made designs of twining leaves and flowers. They could be conveniently glued to blank spaces on walls, and in the 1880s, people had a horror of blank spaces. A taste for the massive monuments of ancient Rome was also prevalent, and a lot of things that recalled the Baths of Diocletian were essayed. They produced ponderous portals of what was confidently supposed to be Roman monumentalness on buildings that were supposed, with even less warrant, to be adaptations of seventeenth-century adaptations of the kind of architecture favored by the Roman emperors.

Italy, France, Switzerland, Venice, Pompeii, and ancient Rome did not satisfy the insatiable appetite of people who wanted their buildings to be good and exotic. There were several houses in the Turkish Taste—sometimes, interchangeably, called Moorish. Unhappily they have been demolished. The Egypt of the Pharaohs, that most remote ancestor of the American Midwest, left its mark on an entrance to—of all places—the University's Hall of Dentistry.

The age of feudal warfare, which flourished only seven or eight centuries before Iowa City was founded, left more numerous marks, in a bewildering variety of places. Battlements with crenellations (small openings in parapets which permitted people on rooftops safely to shoot arrows or pour molten lead on enemies) appeared on many buildings, especially (rather strangely) on churches; the Presbyterian Church has them. But crenellations never attained anything like the popularity of round towers, capped with slate cones, that had been the key defensive elements in medieval fortresses.

Round, thirteenth-century feudal towers with conical caps, especially when executed in fish-scale shingles as they generally were, may seem in themselves sufficiently strange a sight in Iowa, although Dr. Sigmund Freud might have found a reason for their popularity. What is even stranger is that they were frequently a feature of a style known as "Queen Anne," although it certainly had nothing to do with the reign of Anne Stuart at the beginning of the eighteenth century, which was an age of strict classicism and extreme devotion to the laws of proportion. "Queen Anne" was, in fact, the most strictly American style since the log cabin.

Queen Anne houses usually had shingled walls and even wider verandas than before. They rambled. They had a

At 202 Fairchild Street (shown opposite) a feudal tower, inspired by medieval castles but delicately proportioned and executed in shingles, is attached to a medium-sized Basic American House of Queen Anne character. It illustrates the stupefying mixture of tastes that dominated imaginations in the late nineteenth century. Twentieth-century improvements—plastic siding, the removal of the porch, light pastel colors—add a further dimension to the engaging chaos.

In Old Dental (above), a building deplorably placed to block the view of the north wall of the Old Capitol, the architects went wild and furnished it with portals that recall, loosely, the kind of flanking pilasters that were used in Egypt, a thousand years or so B.C. It was built in 1894.

Less delicate souvenirs of feudal warfare, also executed in shingle, are to be found at 308 and 314 Church Street. Heavier and a little more military-looking than that of the Fairchild Street house, they seem less gratuitous—they belong better—but their origins are not less grotesquely inappropriate. One of them has regrettably lost its peak and its porch; peaks and porches rot easily and are hard to repair, and in any case went very much out of fashion in the twentieth century. The houses date from 1890.

great many dormer windows and chimneys and gables—their most identifiable ancestor seems to be the House of the Seven Gables in Salem, Massachusetts (built long before Queen Anne came to the throne), which was the setting of Nathaniel Hawthorne's novel published in 1851. They were comfortable, informal, and handsome, and while they were judged especially appropriate for seashore resorts they appeared in large numbers everywhere.

It is surprising that they should have included towers borrowed from medieval fortifications, which were wholly unknown in both Queen Anne's England and the Salem of the witch-hunts. More surprising still, the towers sometimes incorporated loggias.

The loggia, a sort of balcony or upstairs porch which was, and is, almost standard in Italy, had made its American appearance earlier, in connection with houses in the Italian Taste. It had been used since in all sorts of strange settings; it was practical and pleasant, like the veranda, and it offered rich opportunities for the kind of ornamental woodwork without which no house was complete. Extraordinarily fine loggias appear at 513 Summit Street, on what is perhaps the finest and best preserved of all the Victorian houses on that wonderful street-museum, and on two similar houses on Johnson Street. But these are tame compared to the loggia incorporated *into* a shingled feudal tower in the marvelous "Queen Anne" Musser House. It is astounding, this blending of Puritan Massachusetts with the France of Saint Louis and the Rome of the Borgias, but it is by no means unique. There are several others like it. What is even more astounding is that the blend is harmonious. The almost childlike playing with styles and building materials often came out that way.

But not always. In the second half of the nineteenth century, technology and marketing methods were sufficiently developed that the sale of "pattern books"—collections of designs and blueprints for people planning to build houses—had become big business on a national scale. In the 1890s, one firm, George F. Barber and Co. of Knoxville, Tennessee, was distributing a 172-page catalogue from which customers could select a design, order blueprints, and save themselves the expense of hiring an architect. One customer built such a mail-order house at the corner of College and Summit Streets, in what presumably was judged to be the most marketable taste of the '90s. It is gorgeously unrestrained; French Renaissance themes mingle with carpenter Gothic and fish-scale shingles. Brick and frame and stone stand side by side. A domed octagonal tower suggests the great houses of Elizabethan England, and a huge chimney pierced by a sort of arched picture window suggests nothing that ever existed before or since. At least three other houses built to the same plan are known to survive, in Oregon, in Texas,

At 444 and 504 South Johnson Street, a pair of houses of a conception rather similar to the great house at 513 Summit Street, but of lesser pretension, are similarly equipped with token loggias—far too small to permit the occupants to take the air on them.

Loggias on the magnificent house at 513 Summit Street, built in 1883. Its inspirations are very diverse: classical, Italian, traces of French and Gothic. But their very multiplicity, together with the fact that they are skillfully fitted in to strong, dominant structural patterns, assures the triumph of Shape over Silliness. The details do not intrude. The house has preserved, alone on Summit Street, the iron fence that was so general a feature of more opulent neighborhoods and was important in drawing a line between privacy and the prevailing prospect of a public park.

The Musser House, at 715 College Street, was built in 1890, at the height of the Queen Anne rage. It looks rambling, but this is an optical illusion; actually its fundamental plan is the simple, familiar Basic American, this time not a rectangle, cube, or L, but a cross. The tower is medieval in origin; the loggia was a staggeringly incongruous added amenity. The Musser House and another very like it at 1063 Woodlawn Avenue achieve dignity and a surprising atmosphere of tranquil comfort despite their varied and incompatible inspirations.

Summit Street (above and overleaf). Far and away the handsomest residential street in Iowa City, it powerfully recalls both the pretensions and the accomplishments of the nineteenth-century middle class with its skill at getting what it wanted in the way of dignity, comfort, and serenity. And, supremely, it shows the way in which the right setting can provide a harmony for houses—and individuals—themselves inharmonious, and can, as much as the art, literature, and architecture of an age, convey its inner meaning and nature. Summit Street, as a monument to a particular culture, must—as a street—be judged an important work of art.

The house at 935 East College Street (opposite and p. 43) was built in 1893 from mail order plans sold at a cost of $5.00. Madly eclectic, combining in random profusion ten or twelve entirely different schools of design, and very badly proportioned, it excites the fascination that often attaches to unselfconscious absurdity.

and in North Carolina. When one compares them to Plum Grove, it is easy to understand why Henry Adams worried about what American culture was coming to.

But even so peculiar a whimsy as this fitted in, somehow, with the setting of a well-to-do, unselfconscious, comfortable middle-class street. Victorian houses may individually be curiosities, but when a Victorian street survives in anything like its original form, the unities of the culture that produced it form an evident harmony. There are several places in Iowa City where the amenities of this lost age may be recaptured: parts of Kirkwood Avenue and College Street and, supremely, on Summit Street. Many of its houses are of a later day and many of the old ones have been modernized, but the big lots, the wide and shaded avenue, the dignified seclusion, the sense of space and serenity, all these triumph-

antly embody what people of the late nineteenth century thought was the best of all possible worlds.

There was a great deal more to the harmony than the complacency of a new bourgeoisie. Streets of very modest dwellings, like those of Goosetown, repeat the dignity, the order, the serenity and solid comfort, on a smaller scale. And, in fact, the distinction between the poor streets and the rich ones is of size alone. It was all one culture; the houses and lots of the rich were bigger, but they were in no important way otherwise different. And all, under their varied decorations, were the same kind of house, simple cubes or rectangles that correspond to the unifying thrift and common sense of a community that had no aristocracy, no members who did not work, and to the hard necessities of the Iowa climate. The dark cool rooms with high ceilings, the wide porches shaded by great elms, where citizens might recline in that

House at 1212 Rochester Road (right). The fine proportions of this small house, the skillful arrangement of porch and gable, and the simple decoration on the eaves give it a dignity, almost an elegance, that puts it in the same class as the much grander and costlier houses of the rich. It is a legacy of the pervading atmosphere of comfort, serenity, and amenity that united the residential quarters of varied income levels in a pleasant harmony in the late nineteenth century.

particularly American contrivance, the rocking chair, while sipping innocent lemonade and conversing with neighbors passing on the sidewalk, these provided a classless summer idyll until the telephone, the automobile, the cocktail, and the air-conditioner wrecked it. The Victorian houses, for all their variety in opulence and style, were Basic American.

By the end of the century, Basic American had evolved into a style very definitely its own, a model for half the farmhouses in Iowa and for many surviving houses in the towns. The gable, the porch, the frame construction, the taste for space, and for economy, provided a standard for everybody. The Midwest had found its idiom, produced an architecture, and fulfilled its promise and its destiny.

The promise and destiny were drastic social mobility and an underlying sense of equality. The men of substance in the days of easy money had tried, and failed, to build a gentry; they were, after all, glovers, linseed oil manufacturers, brick-layers, and carpenters who had done well. Snobbery put down no roots. By the end of the century equality had produced its own monuments.

From borrowings and imitations, from frauds and fads, from miscalculations and mistakes, and from the underlying good sense that dictated uninterrupted adherence to a simple and native-born basic building, there emerged by the end of the nineteenth century a kind of domestic architecture entirely original and entirely Midwestern, a frame house with wide porches and gables, and with only superficial variations of ornament and detail. At 128 Fairchild Street, at the corner of Dubuque Street (left), stands one of the clearest, and handsomest, examples of a paradigm house, born of varied ancestors but admirably adapted to the physical requirements of the Iowa climate and the spiritual and aesthetic requirements of what Meredith Willson called "the Iowa way."

By 1900, two very different and conflicting new tendencies were evident in the design of buildings. They would eventually modify and then destroy the native kind of house that the late nineteenth century had borne. The first was the school of design that was known as Modern and would later be called Functional. It arose from the reasonable notion that the structure of a building ought to be the chief element of its form and appearance. In an age of structural steel the use of, say, medieval decorations that had originally been determined by the needs of stone and wood was absurd, the Modernists said. If a doorway were set in a stone arch, the arch ought to be emphatic. If a building were built of structural steel, then the frame should form the aesthetic theme. This was essentially a *moral* idea, and Modern architects freely, and sometimes carelessly, talked about "honest" design, loudly denouncing Ruskin's creed that architecture was ornament, rather illogically ridiculing his statement that Gothic was the "Architecture of Truth."

The precursors of Modern Architecture were not inclined to reject traditional styles; what they rejected was a meretricious application of them to buildings that had nothing in common structurally with the originals. One of the finest of the precursors of Modernism was Henry Hobson Richardson. He admired the heavy, plain buildings called Romanesque, whose outward details had provided the inspiration for the Presbyterian Church and Saint Mary's. But he saw not the details, the round arched windows and the battlements; he saw solutions to difficult problems of engineering, massive buildings where arches were required to support walls, not applied as frivolous afterthought. His followers, less sophisticated but no less sedulously devoted to his principles, began to build Midwestern courthouses and churches and railroad stations in the 1880s. The Johnson County Courthouse is a good example of their work, with its massiveness, its emphatic arches and thick masonry, its sparse decoration. Blank spaces, beams and lintels, and buttresses were coming back into fashion. The Courthouse is imposing, solid, even majestic. And it marked the way toward the age when structural engineering would engulf every other aspect of design.

The second trend noticeable by the turn of the century led in a very different direction. It flowered sooner, eclipsed Modern Architecture for a time, and then died in Depression and War. It was a pendulum swing, perhaps merely the rebellion of a new generation, that resurrected Republican Simplicity and Georgian ideals. For as the new century opened simplicity was in fashion again. There were patriotic overtones; America was old enough now to conclude that glory was to be found not only in foreign models but in its

The Johnson County Courthouse, built in 1901 from the plans of A. William Russ, of Grand Rapids, Michigan, was intended to commemorate the prosperity and the civic spirit of the community and the majesty of democratic government. It is very assertive indeed, and its huge, rough-cut stones, its slightly top-heavy tower, its pretentious portal, seem to some people today impractical and frankly ugly. Others find it impressive, and seen from a distance, from the hills across the river, it rises with something of the same gigantic symbolism as an Old-World cathedral dominating its surrounding town. This was what its architect presumably intended, but he intended something else, more novel and important: the first stirring of a reborn notion that buildings ought to be "honest," that in appearance they should reveal and indeed flaunt the structural elements that make possible high walls, arched windows, and soaring towers.

In the 1890s the Classic Revival began. It appeared first in the form of another style adapted from the past, that of the monumental buildings of imperial Rome. In most such Romanoid buildings the varied textures, the elaborate details, and the grandiose shapes of late Victorian design were still very noticeable. But presently the designs would merge with those inspired by the enthusiasm for reborn Georgian. In the house at 624 South Summit Street, built in the early 90s, the rebirth of the Georgian tradition is prophe- sied. The air of massiveness, like the large plate glass windows, is still very nineteenth century, but the siding is red brick—the Georgian trade- mark—instead of clapboard and shingles as in the contemporary Roman house shown on p. 56. Ornament is fairly low-keyed, and there is some effort at architectural balance. Symmetry and coherence are about to resume their long ascendancy, and within ten years the houses of the '70s and '80s will be called "hideous" by the younger generation.

own rich Colonial and Federal past. Second-hand, Greece came back into style; towers, fancy woodwork, and medieval- ism went out. Ceilings began, although slowly, to descend, from fifteen feet towards seven and a half. White paint, unseen for half a century or more, reappeared.

It was white paint that wrought the greatest outward change. Victorians had liked what they thought of as "rich" colors: chocolate and dark green, terracotta, crimson and burnt orange, buff, maroon, and even puce. Now all wooden surfaces were being painted ivory or frosty white. This was thought—especially when combined with red brick—to be particularly "Colonial" (although actually exterior woodwork in the eighteenth century had generally been painted a sort of pale khaki, which was the nearest thing to white that chemists then could provide in the way of weatherproof paint).

But beneath the paint there was still continuity. The new "Colonial" houses, increasingly numerous by 1910, looked more like the houses of 1890 than those of 1770. Victorian traditions lingered, in the form of porches and turned wood- work. The Greek laws of proportion were not re-learned. And there was continuity, too, in the persisting fondness for im- itation. Patriotic Greek and Colonial might dominate, but there was competition from other "styles." The models,

The house at 304 South Summit Street shows clearly the capacity of the sensible Basic House of the nineteenth century to survive changes in fashion. Levi Kauffman, a real estate developer, built it in the early 1880s, with the basic, simple plan inherited from the earlier decades and Italian decoration of a sort already, by then, regarded as a little old-fashioned. Originally it was of red brick, lavishly draped with wooden ornament: heavy eaves with grotto-like bracketing and pendants, and a large, fancily-turned veranda.

A half a century later, the veranda suffered the fate of so many of its kind, the brick was painted white, and a neo-classical doorway was added. All this was done to adapt it to the Colonial taste that was so popular in the first half of the twentieth century. But the ornamental eaves and the big, Victorian plate glass windows survive, and it is a tribute to the solidity of the original design that they live in dignity with the Colonial remodeling.

Ardenia (above and right), at 925 Kirkwood Avenue, is the exact opposite of the ideal of "honest" design so ponderously illustrated in the Courthouse. Its lowering, castle-like facade was added to an ordinary frame house. The wild and savage atmosphere of primitive warriors fighting meaningless battles with bows and arrows in the wilderness is greatly enhanced by the overgrown shrubbery and a decaying brick wall that surround it.

however, were very different. Grandeur and richness were decidedly going out. Coziness, even cuteness, was coming in. And so, until the triumph of Functionalism in the 1940s, people continued to experiment in ways to make the Basic American House look like something else. The imitations were frequently more studied and less imaginative and lively than in the nineteenth century. A good deal of the neo-Georgian and "English" building between 1910 and 1940 was singularly sterile. Some of the other twentieth-century styles were more vigorous.

Vigorous, and peculiar. In the mid-1920s a hotelman named Albert Burkley bought a house which had originally been built in 1855 by the son of Governor Lucas. It was a conventional frame house of that period, with Italian details, but Burkley added a sort of medieval fortress in brick, complete with crenellations and turrets. The fortress was only skin deep, a facade attached to the old house. Another note of beguiling idiocy is another addition at the rear, in a vaguely Georgian style, so that Ardenia, as the place is called, displays three entirely different phases of taste, each more or less borrowed from a different era of the remote past.

Ardenia is idiosyncratic. There is nothing like it anywhere in Iowa City, or elsewhere for the matter of that. Scarcely less surprising, but much more representative of prevailing tastes, were extraordinary little cottages of fairy-tale dimensions and flavor. Some of them—inspired perhaps by the great popularity of *The Wind in the Willows,* a whimsy of anthropomorphic toads and moles—appeared in stone clusters that look like housing developments for gnomes. But most of the imitations were more orthodox. Half-timbering was a primitive kind of construction, used in northern Europe until better methods were perfected, in which a framework of heavy beams was filled in with rubble or rough brick and plastered over, leaving the beams exposed. In the twentieth century, half-timbering recurred in a fraudulent form of decoration externally applied and was called Olde English (in Great Britain, Stockbroker's Tudor). Today, obsolete but not unappealing, it strikes an odd note on a street of Basic American houses.

Other, sometimes less unsuitable, English models were imitated. (Although there is one house in Iowa City that has an imitation thatched roof, perhaps the less said about that, the better.) In the last half of the eighteenth century the Adam brothers were the most fashionable architects in Great Britain. They perfected a new form of Georgian design; what had, in its origins, been strong and massive became elegant, gay, and somewhat trivial. Adam buildings are light, highly decorated with woodcarving and leaden

Even more "dishonest" than skin-deep fortresses and elfin cottages, from the standpoint of the now reigning morality of Modern Architecture, was the short-lived American taste for Olde English houses. They were just ordinary houses with excessively steep-pitched roofs and some fake half-timbering glued on. They have become curiosities in the day of the low-slung ranch house. But they do, sometimes, recall both the real thing, the half-timbered villages found from the northern edges of Norway and England to the villages of Normandy, and the phase of American taste when it was thought desirable to combine the outer aspect of places that sheltered primitive but ingenious people with the inner convenience of central heating and powder rooms.

There are several clusters of little stone cottages with cozy dimensions, pebbly walls, and meaningless little projections. Here the picture is what matters; an illusion is intended. The science of the Strength of Materials is replaced by a fairytale, to the point where one almost expects to see talking bunny rabbits and elves flitting through the little gardens. Charm, too sedulously sought, is not quite attained. This group is in the 1300 block of Muscatine Avenue.

The facade of a building which, on the ground floor, now houses Seifert's and The Stable, clothiers, at 10-12 South Clinton Street. Its upper stories, with pediment and pilasters, give a fairly accurate idea of the graceful and slightly effete elegance of the architecture of the late eighteenth century in England.

The President's House, 102 Church Street, has a superb view over the valley of the Iowa, and a regal presence. Its ostentatious neo-Georgian exterior is a trifle awkward, as were many of the early twentieth-century efforts to re-create the great houses of the Colonial era. It seems slightly alien to that most egalitarian of all American institutions, a state university. It was built in 1908.

designs in windows, often equipped with pilasters—flat columns built into a wall—and exquisitely proportioned. Not many twentieth-century builders were able successfully to match the airy beauty of Adam facades, but one fine one was achieved above a shop front on Clinton Street.

On the other hand, the stronger and more solemn version of Georgian, which gave America Independence Hall, Mount Vernon, and Monticello, had hundreds of imitators. Some were reasonably successful, although Mount Vernon, naturally the most popular model, lends itself indifferently to reinterpretation on a small lot. Some were less than exact facsimiles of the great eighteenth-century originals. The University President's House, a very early and pretentious example of neo-Georgian (in its loosest sense), features a square portico with heavy columns topped by large urns,

showing that grandeur was not entirely out of fashion and that Georgian buildings *might* be clumsy if they strayed far enough from their models.

The last stage of the great classical tradition in England, before it was lost in the Gothic revival in the early nineteenth century, was Regency, a style rather approximately associated with the years 1810-1820, when the future George IV was Regent for his demented father. Regency houses were likely to be compact, rigorously symmetrical, and somewhat stiffly refined. Some were fancifully ornate, some severely plain. Of the latter sort, one good example was built in 1941 in Iowa City. Just as the original Regency houses were the last to be built in the great classical tradition of the eighteenth century, this one was the last to be built in the classic revival that began in the 1890s. A cycle had repeated itself.

A very different stage of English cultural history is recalled in this chastely
dignified Regency House at 354 Ferson Street, built in 1941. In a simplified
way it quite accurately recalls the polite formality of the time of Jane Austen.
Everything is in its place. There is nothing unnecessary, nothing emotional,
nothing evocative. The Age of Reason had reached its final and rather chilly
expression at the beginning of the nineteenth century; thinkers were just
beginning to feel that Reason was neither sufficient nor entirely real, and
by way of reaction, wild, romantic emotions and puritanical moral principles
were about to come into style again. They would produce the excesses of the
Victorian world that impended.

Not only England was rifled for models. In the years after the first world war affluence and self-confidence again flowered in America on almost the scale—but with more discipline—as in the post-Civil War years, and so did the yearning for imported atmospheres. France was also looked to—not now the France of the showy and vulgar Second Empire but the France of rustic manor houses and country cottages. On Park Street is a house that attempted to re-create the atmosphere of a whole European peasant village, one that is more Norman-French than anything else. To a remarkable degree it succeeds; of all the twentieth-century imitations it is the most evocative and the most charming, and—at least from a little distance—the most authentic.

It was the University fraternities, riding high in those years, that built the largest and most elaborate imitations. They needed space and they had the money. There are Mount Vernons, Haddon Halls, Roman Villas, Gothic monasteries, all on a grand scale. A few are very interesting. One Florentine Villa recalls with surprising realism the glories of the High Renaissance. Several English buildings, some with quite genuine-looking English stonework and good proportions, and some with fake half-timbering, cluster in tiers above the left bank of the Iowa and re-create a pleasant and almost believable picture of an English town. Facing them is the most interesting of all, a quite convincing French *manoir* or country house of the early sixteenth century, spendidly surveying the river.

The University itself underwent architectural vicissitudes of a sort comparable to those of domestic buildings and the fraternities. It had, after it expanded beyond the narrow walls of the Old Capitol, a considerable array of Victorian academic halls, several of them of the Charles Addams sort. Most have disappeared now. Then, in the 1890s, came the Greek Revival, with the reborn, and not altogether absurd, conviction that it was proper to emphasize the link between the modern university and the academies of Athens by building very large classroom buildings of Greek design, if not on a Greek scale. Four of them, far too big for the site, were built around the Old Capitol, to form what its makers hoped would be a classical unity called the Pentacrest. The two that face Clinton Street are almost twins; Schaeffer, built in 1898, and Macbride, finished in 1905, have monumental classical fronts with Ionic columns and pediments imaginatively decorated with stone flora and fauna. They achieve a sort of oversized majesty.

The best thing on the Pentacrest, however, aside from the Old Capitol itself, is the terrace above the river, on the west side. Here the evocation is not of Greece but of Versailles (where Greece had also been a source of inspiration). Heavy

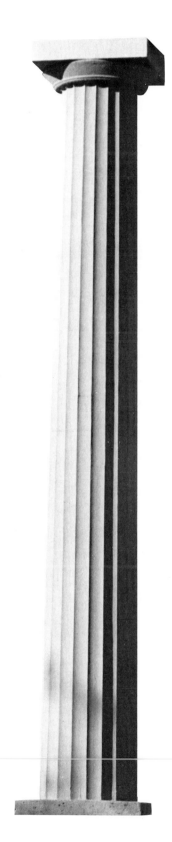

In the nineteenth century people liked imitations of nature; ladies made artificial moss and had floral designs on their carpets and window hangings, and wooden leaves and tendrils twined around their sofas and their porch pillars. People who were really in touch with nature, like French peasants, had no taste or money for such fancies. They were obliged to accept and understand their surroundings, to use the materials that nature provided, and to build in ways that guarded against danger and damage from natural forces. The old houses of rural France are nothing if not functional, with low, thick stone walls, heavy roofs to ward off rain and snow, and unplanned wings and outbuildings and walled yards, so that isolated farms often form little villages. In a world of steam-heated suburbs, such concessions to reality looked quaint, and quaintness was conquered and captured in this re-created Old World farm at 524 Park Street, built in the early 1930s. It represents Escape. It is a nice Escape; despite its very Midwestern verdure it smells strongly of France, which is a pleasant place to escape to.

The Phi Beta Pi House, at 109 River Street, was built in 1929. The stone walls and wide eaves and fine proportions are quite authentic reminders of the kind of country house that was built 500 years ago in central Italy, where the sun is very hot, the memory of ancient Rome very strong, and the understanding of art very deep.

The Phi Kappa Sigma House (above), built in 1931 facing the river at 716 North Dubuque Street, has handsome walls of dressed stone, and its windows and gables are "correct" replicas of buildings in England in the late Middle Ages. It is very proper and academic, and it shows very clearly to a stay-at-home traveler what an English manor house in—say—Gloucestershire, built in—say—the fifteenth century, looked like.

Brooding on its hilltop, the Delta Chi House (opposite), at 309 North Riverside Drive, is a slightly menacing but extremely accurate re-creation of a French manor house of the seventeenth century—built in the late 1920s. The high mansards, the stucco walls, the brick dressings, the graceful shapes of doors and windows, even the little round tower (a sort of hangover from the fortifications of much earlier days of disorder before the introduction of gunpowder) are all exactly right; the setting, perhaps, is wrong, and the building looks as a result like something displayed in a museum; still, it is not only instructively authentic but beautiful.

The west terrace of the Old Capitol.

The individual fraternity houses along North Dubuque Street (opposite), mostly from the 1920s, some of dressed stone, some half-timbered, and some of Georgian or Italian style, are mostly not in themselves very interesting or appealing. But taken together, with the hill and the river and the ducks, they compose a most attractive picture, decidedly Old World in flavor. It is a comment on the rather sterile architecture of the '20s, when Victorian originality and bold experiments had given way to attempts at more exact imitations of Old-World models, that such buildings look more attractive when different styles are mixed together and viewed from a distance.

balustrades, grand staircases, greenery, a slightly forced formality, and the sense of how best to use topography to form vistas, provide a dignified pleasance for agreeable leisure.

The awareness of their ancestry in ancient Athens was soon forgotten by the people who decided what the University should look like. By the 1900s there was spreading westward from Princeton and Bryn Mawr the belief, expensively embodied in masonry, that all academic buildings ought to look like Oxford, or at least like what Americans thought Oxford looked like. This meant in practice imitating a variety of models, since Oxford was very various in dates and designs. Most popular were the medieval Oxford colleges like Magdalen, which recalled the ancient connection between learning and the Christian Church (the considerably more ancient connection between learning and pagan Athens having gone out of style). In the 1920s, sketchy re-creations of Magdalen Tower appeared on half the campuses in the country (they also appeared on warehouses and department stores, to which they were thought to add a certain respectability). Iowa City, fortunately, has only one important sample of this fad, a rather clumsy openwork bell-tower (without bells, of course) atop the University General Hospital. Another kind of model was provided by the brick buildings of the sixteenth century, and the rage for Tudor dormitories did not entirely pass the University by either. A few stone details—window-frames and doorways—of more or less accurate Elizabethan design were attached to very large and rather factory-like brick dormitories. The Psychopathic Hospital is a quite authentic reproduction of buildings from the age of Henry VIII.

Depression, war, and an increasing acceptance of Modern Architecture put an end to such fancies. The Chicago Modernists won at last a decisive victory, although it was probably due more to economics than to their theories of art. Their insistence that architecture was largely a matter of engineering, their enthusiasm for reinforced concrete and structural steel, allowed a much cheaper kind of construction than anything involving classical columns or Gothic towers. Their insistence that convenience was a criterion of beauty— and that ornament and tradition were irrelevant to it—furnished a moral and artistic justification for saving the money.

The authors of Modernism, Frank Lloyd Wright and Louis Sullivan, were geniuses. Most of their followers were not, and some of their followers' followers were lacking in elementary good sense. Modern Architecture became, as often as not, shoddily bleak, and it must be said that The University of Iowa has had more than its fair share of shoddy bleakness. In the 1950s, when people were becoming

Doorway of Woodlawn, the former Nurses' Dormitory, on Glenview Avenue. It is the kind of doorway that was being widely built on large houses and public buildings in late sixteenth- and early seventeenth-century England. The English had borrowed it from Italy, where such doorways were common during the period of the Renaissance, which inspired, and indeed revolutionized, the life and culture of all of Europe. The most notable feature of the Italian Renaissance was the rediscovery of themes and models from the ancient world, after the long dominance of medieval ideas and design. The models for such doorways as this come from the most luxurious and decadent days of the Roman Empire. It is, in short, a pleasant, expensive, and rather silly copy of a copy of a copy.

The University Psychopathic Hospital, on Newton Road, built in 1920. It reflects the Tudor (sixteenth-century English) sort of design popular at the time for schools, churches, hospitals, and shops. Casements, bay-windows, ornamental sandstone dressings, chimneys, steep-pitched roofs, little dormers, and construction in rose-colored brick, are all sufficiently authentic to mitigate the quite untypical expanse of blank wall and the rather slick, overtidy design.

In very sharp contrast to the immensely long tradition that lies behind the doorway of Woodlawn is the modernity of the College of Nursing (opposite), dramatically constructed on a bluff on the right bank of the Iowa in 1972. It owes little to any past model; it is the product of concrete and steel structure, which have been used only in the last 100 years. Here twentieth-century architecture is at its best, or at least its most imposing. It is original, imaginative, and most important of all it takes the greatest possible advantage of its site.

The College of Dentistry (above), like the College of Nursing, has no ancestors. Built in 1973, it was very much made in and for our time, with emphasis on Mass, Shape, and Material. The faint symbolic suggestion of gigantic teeth may be a fancy of the beholder, not of the architect; but it is certainly not without warrant or precedent—one of the greatest of Modern architects saw fit to design the TWA Terminal at Kennedy Airport in the likeness of a gigantic winged insect.

aware of the pitfalls of building great cubes of bare brick, a most ill-judged effort was made to "relieve" bleakness by the use of shiny plastic panels, often of relentless blues and greens—Hillcrest Dormitory and the College of Law being regrettable memorials to such efforts. In the 1960s, however, this school of Modern, which may best be entitled Alleviated Factory, gave way to an entirely new one called (even by its practitioners) Brutal. Brutality involved large geometric masses with surfaces of bare, rough concrete. Mitigation of brutality was sought through the manipulation of structural masses in the correct belief that light and shadow are a form of decoration that dramatizes, if it does not soften, harsh lines and textures. The manipulation of masses was practiced with handsome effect in Saint Thomas More. It is displayed with majesty in the College of Nursing, where the

masses include, happily, the bluff on which it stands above the river. It is displayed with what looks like weird humor in the College of Dentistry, whose masses are contrived to suggest the outlines of gigantic molars.

Whatever one may think of these vast exercises in pure Shape, there is no doubt that they have vitality. In this they contrast to the designs, both Pseudo-Oxonian and Alleviated Factory, that preceded them. The contrast between the weak and foolish belfry of the General Hospital and the adjacent, thoroughly Modern, parking ramp is the contrast between folly and function.

Sometimes, particularly in small buildings, Modernists attain a more human effect with stunning success, conceivably as often as—although certainly no oftener than—the builders of any other age. In Iowa City the masterpiece of the

91

It would be difficult to find a more illuminating juxtaposition than the neo-Gothic tower of the General Hospital, dating from 1927, and the parking ramp beside it, symbols of a drastic change in American culture and ideals that took place in the middle of the twentieth century. The tower represents the fancies of an age and a nation sufficiently immature, in the first half of the century, to find solace in imitating churches of medieval England; the parking ramp symbolizes the America of the second half of the century, the America of technology triumphant, acknowledging no debts and no exotic heritage, ruthlessly efficient, assured, handsome, and relentlessly original.

Modern buildings are not always ruthless; it is appropriate to strike an encouraging note with the beautiful Iowa State Bank and Trust Building on Route 6, designed by Richard Hansen and built in 1969.

In the Middle Ages, when glass was irregular and brittle, windows were made of small bits of it fitted into a wooden lattice. Diagonal strips of wood, forming diamond-shaped openings, were found to give the greatest strength and were widely used in the casements of medieval dwellings. As the quality of glass improved, larger panes became possible and the diamond shape was abandoned. Eventually, in the nineteenth century, plate glass was invented, eliminating the need for any panes or lattices at all. But the diamond-shape has been revived in the form of a wooden lattice fitted over a plate-glass window, to decorate that most characteristic achievement of domestic architecture in the second half of the twentieth century, the "ranch house." The phony medieval flavor thus achieved may be radically deplored by purists and modernists, since it has nothing whatever to do with either the design or the structural needs of the buildings to which it is applied; but, seen in another light, it may be taken as a token of continuity, of a half-conscious awareness of a past that belongs to all of us.

Post-Eclectic Era, as the last 30 years may be called, is a drive-in bank, an artistic triumph not at all inappropriate to a society where automobiles and interest rates count so heavily. It presents itself as convenient, serene, and pleasant; but functionalism here has, too, a tinge of exotic charm, a trace of an influence that may, with a little imagination, be identified as Japanese.

However successful, or however strange and foolish, buildings may look to the casual passerby, they all tell us a great deal about our past and something about ourselves. They may call forth amusement, awe, or sometimes horror, but they should never be looked at with indifference, for they are living—and long-lived—expressions of what people thought was technically feasible, intellectually important, morally proper, artistically worthy, and economically sound. They are human minds, souls, and bodies commemorated in material forms, the spirit of the ages in timber and stone. It is sufficient to compare the Egyptian portal of Old Dental with the concrete molars of New Dental, separated by less than a century, to learn that tastes and beliefs and knowledge are in a state of continuous revolution. It is sufficient to look at the shingled, slated, feudal bastions of the Queen Anne houses to learn that through all revolutions very little changes: it is an awesome testimony to the hold the past has on us that in a Midwestern American town in a New World, in the age of industry, and at a time when knowledge was far greater than had ever been achieved before, people in the nineteenth and twentieth centuries were moved to re-create structures that primitive forebears ingeniously devised to baffle attacking armies armed with arrows and catapults, 800 years before and 4000 miles away.

For nations and towns and individuals are always turning back, just as they are always looking forward. The new architecture is proud of its pure contemporaneity, but it is already forming its own traditions. And it is borrowing them, too. Faint echoes of Japan's classic simplicities are heard in a drive-in bank, and on a ranch house there are casements with diamond-paned windows like those of medieval England. Any street is a picture album of the family of man.

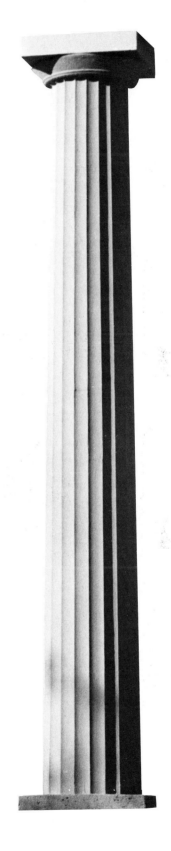

The text of this book is set in ten point Palatino, a twentieth-century typeface designed by Hermann Zapf. Despite its modernity, the type has a classical elegance and graceful proportion. Captions are set in eight point Palatino italic.

The title page is Caslon Antique, first cast about 1897 by Barnhart Brothers & Spindler. Appropriately, it imitates the eighteenth-century cutting of William Caslon, which often became badly worn with long use, especially in America where new fonts were scarce.

Display type is Century Expanded, an adaptation of Century, designed by Linn Boyd Benton and T. L. DeVinne for *Century Magazine* in 1894. The Expanded version was first cut around 1900 to meet Typographical Union standards.

The book was printed on Prentice enamel by Tel-Graphics Corporation of East Dubuque, Illinois. The hardbound volumes were bound by Worzalla Publishing Company, Stevens Point, Wisconsin and the paperbound by Wm. C. Brown Publishing Company of Dubuque, Iowa.

Production staff:
Editing and design—L. Edward Purcell
Copyediting and proofreading — Robert Bower, Henrietta Zagel
Typing—Ingrid McWilliams

The author collaborated with the staff concerning design and lay-out.